HANDLING THE WORD OF TRUTH

Handling the Word of Truth

Law and Gospel in the Church Today

JOHN T. PLESS

CONCORDIA PUBLISHING HOUSE · SAINT LOUIS

Library of Congress Cataloging-in-Publication Data

Pless, John T., 1953–
    Handling the word of truth : law and gospel in the church today / John T. Pless.
      p. cm.
    ISBN 0-7586-0020-8
1. Law and gospel. 2. Lutheran Church-Doctrines. I. Title.
    BT79.P54 2005
    241'.2—dc22

                                                    2004018685

2 3 4 5 6 7 8 9 10   13 12 11 10 09 08 07

CONTENTS

PREFACE

It has been well over a hundred years since Dr. C. F. W. Walther (1811–1887) delivered a series of Friday evening lectures on the proper distinction between Law and Gospel to the students of Concordia Seminary in St. Louis, Missouri. While cultural circumstances have changed dramatically, the truth of Walther's insight remains constant. In his day, Walther was confronted with challenges to this truth on all sides—from Roman Catholicism, rationalism, pietism, and a multitude of sects. In our day of "ambiguous denominationalism" the challenge is even greater. Ecumenical compromise has blurred the doctrinal lines so much that there is fuzziness even in some Lutheran circles over the centrality of justification by grace through faith alone. Witness the case of the *Joint Declaration on the Doctrine of Justification* issued by the Roman Catholic Church and the Lutheran World Federation in 1999, a theological statement in which the Lutherans compromised everything and the Catholics compromised nothing. A host of cross-denominational movements and books capture the attention of many Lutheran laity at a grassroots level. Promise Keepers, "What Would Jesus Do?" (WWJD?), *The Prayer of Jabez,* and *The Purpose-Driven Life* are notable examples in which the wolf of Reformed dogma sneaks into the Lutheran flock under the sheep's clothing of biblical principles for living.

We live in a decaying culture where good is called evil and evil good. Marriage is severely attacked, while homosexuality is held up as an acceptable "lifestyle." Personal and public integrity seems to have evaporated. Basic moral assumptions are questioned and in many cases rejected in the name of tolerance and diversity. Christians in such an age confront a twofold temptation. On one hand, there is increasing pressure for the church to conform itself to the spirit of the times. Attempts are made to redefine God's Law or make its boundaries elastic. The commandments of God are seen as general principles, not as a Word from God that convicts and condemns sin. On the other hand, there is the temptation for Christians to focus on morality. The chief aim of the church is thought to be producing a culture that runs counter to that of our world, a culture defined by biblical values. The Gospel is pressed into the service of the Law. It becomes a means to morality, not a word from God that forgives sin for Jesus' sake.

The only change that the Law can work is death. The Law does not merely scold; it kills. It closes off every path that the sinner would use in a vain attempt to escape God. Where the Law does not find its end in Christ (see Romans 10:4), it will lead either to pride or despair. Such a mishandling of the Law in preaching or in witness leads to what Luther calls a "Turk's faith." In a 1532 sermon on Galatians 3:23–24, Luther says:

> For that reason their faith is, to say the best, purely and simply a Turk's faith which stands solely upon the bare letter of the Law and on outward acts of doing or not doing, such as "You shall not kill" and "You shall not steal." They take the view that the Law is satisfied if a man does not use his fist for homicide, does not steal anyone's property, and the like. In short, they believe that sort of external piety is a righteousness that prevails before God. But such doctrine and faith are false and wrong, even though the works performed are themselves good and have been commanded by God.[1]

The Gospel alone has the power to forgive sins and make alive the heart that is dead to God. This is why Walther insisted that the Gospel must always predominate in Christian preaching and witness.

This book takes Walther's twenty-five theses on the proper distinction of Law and Gospel, organizes them under thirteen headings, and unpacks them using insights from Walther's own exposition of the theses, as well as materials from Luther and some contemporary Lutheran thinkers. Readers may wish to study this book in tandem with Walther's *The Proper Distinction between Law and Gospel* because it is frequently referenced throughout these pages. Questions for reflection and discussion are included at the end of each chapter for personal or group use.

In many ways this book is the culmination of pastoral work with students at Valparaiso University (1979–1983) and the University of Minnesota (1983–2000). The necessity of Walther's distinction of Law and Gospel has been reinforced in my current calling as teacher of future pastors at Concordia Theological Seminary in Ft. Wayne, Indiana. I am grateful to my students—both past and present—without whose perceptive questions and insights this book would not have been possible. I am especially indebted to the good people of Zion Lutheran Church in Ft. Wayne, Indiana, who listened and reacted to each of these chapters in the adult Bible class in the autumn and winter of 2003–2004. I dedicate this book to my parents, for it was from their lips that I first heard God's Law and Gospel.

JOHN T. PLESS
EPIPHANY 2004

NOTES

1. Martin Luther, "The Distinction between Law and Gospel: A Sermon by Martin Luther," trans. Willard L. Burce, *Concordia Journal* 18 (April 1992): 154. Also see appendix.

Chapter One

Two Different Doctrines

The doctrinal contents of the entire Holy Scriptures, both of the Old and the New Testament, are made up of two doctrines differing fundamentally from each other, viz., the Law and the Gospel.—C. F. W. Walther (Thesis I [Walther, 6])

The true knowledge of the distinction between the Law and the Gospel is not only a glorious light, affording the correct understanding of the entire Holy Scriptures, but without this knowledge Scripture is and remains a sealed book.— C. F. W. Walther (Thesis IV [Walther, 60])

Critics of Christianity have long tried to discredit the faith by attempting to locate differences between various biblical authors. However, they have missed the supreme difference within the Scriptures that Walther points to in his first thesis. God speaks in two fundamentally different ways. He speaks a word of Law that threatens sinners with divine punishment, delivers wrath, and brings death and condemnation. Yet He also speaks a word of Gospel that promises grace to undeserving sinners, bestows forgiveness of sins, and delivers life and salvation. The distinction between these two words of God is nowhere better summarized than in Romans 3 where the apostle Paul writes:

For by works of the law no human being will be justified in His sight, since through the law comes knowledge of sin. But now the righteousness of God has been manifested apart from the law, although the Law and the Prophets bear witness to it—the righteousness of God through faith in Jesus Christ for all who believe. For there is no distinction: for all have sinned and fall short of the glory of God, and are justified by His grace as a gift, through the redemption that is in Christ Jesus, whom God put forward as a propitiation by His blood, to be received by faith. (Romans 3:20–25a)

The purity of the Gospel's proclamation hinges on the distinction between Law and Gospel. James Nestingen observes:

When Law and Gospel are improperly distinguished, both are undermined. Separated from the Law, the Gospel gets absorbed into an ideology of tolerance in which indiscriminateness is equated with grace. Separated from the Gospel, the Law becomes an insatiable demand hammering away at the conscience until it destroys a person.

When Law and Gospel are properly distinguished, however, both are established. The Law can be set forth in its full-scale demand, so that it lights the way to order and through the work of the Spirit drives us to Christ. The Gospel can be declared in all of its purity, so that forgiveness of sins and deliverance from the powers of death and the devil are bestowed in the presence of our crucified and risen Lord.[1]

To distinguish Law from Gospel, one must know how they are different.

Walther observes that Law and Gospel differ in six ways. First, the Law differs from the Gospel by the manner in which it is revealed. The Law is inscribed in the human heart, and though it is dulled by sin, the conscience bears witness to its truth (Romans 2:14–15). "The Ten Commandments were published only for the purpose of bringing out in bold outline the dulled script of the original Law written in men's hearts" (Walther, 8). That is why the moral teachings of non-Christian religions are essentially the same as those found in the Bible. Yet it is different with the Gospel. The Gospel can never be known from the conscience. It is not a word from within the heart; it comes from outside. It comes from Christ alone. "All religions contain portions of the Law. Some of the heathen, by their knowledge of the Law, have advanced so far that they have even perceived the necessity of an inner cleansing of the soul, a purification of the thoughts and desires. But of the Gospel not a particle is found anywhere except in the Christian religion" (Walther, 8). The fact that humanity is alienated from God, in need of cleansing and reconciliation, is a theme common to many belief systems. It is only Christianity that teaches that God Himself justifies the ungodly.

Second, the Law is distinct from the Gospel in regard to content. The Law can only make demands. It tells us what we must do, but it is impotent to redeem us from its demands (Galatians 3:12–14). The Law speaks to our works, always showing that even the best of them are tainted with the fingerprints of our sin and insufficient for salvation. The Gospel contains no demand, only the gift of God's grace and truth in Christ. It has nothing to say about works of human achievement and everything to say about the mercy of God for sinners. "The Law tells us what we are to do. No such instruction is contained in the Gospel. On the contrary, the Gospel reveals to us only what God is doing. The Law is speaking concerning our works; the Gospel, concerning the great works of God" (Walther, 9).

Third, the Law and the Gospel differ in the promises that each make. The Law offers great good to those who keep its demands. Think what life would be like in a world where the Ten Commandments were perfectly kept. Imagine a universe where God was feared, loved, and trusted above all things and the neighbor was loved so selflessly that there would be no murder, adultery, theft, lying, or coveting. Indeed, such a world would be paradise. This is what the Law promises. There is only the stipulation that we obey its commands. Do the Law and you will live, says Holy Scripture

(Leviticus 18:5; Luke 10:25–28). The Gospel, by contrast, makes a promise without demand or condition. It is a word from God that does not cajole or manipulate but simply gives and bestows what it says, namely, the forgiveness of sins. Luther defined the Gospel as "a preaching of the incarnate Son of God, given to us without any merit on our part for salvation and peace. It is a word of salvation, a word of grace, a word of comfort, a word of joy, a voice of the bridegroom and the bride, a good word, a word of peace."[2] This is the word that the church is to proclaim throughout the world (Mark 16:15–16). It is the message that salvation is not achieved but received by grace through faith alone (Ephesians 2:8–9). The Gospel is a word that promises blessing to those who are cursed, righteousness to the unrighteous, and life to the dead.

Fourth, Law and Gospel are distinct when it comes to threats. Walther puts it simply: "The Gospel contains no threats at all, but only words of consolation. Wherever in Scripture you come across a threat, you may be assured that that passage belongs in the Law" (Walther, 11). The Law threatens sinners with punishment, pronouncing a curse on all who fail to live up to its requirements (Deuteronomy 27:26). The Gospel announces forgiveness for those crushed by the threat of the Law, for Christ Jesus came into the world to rescue the unrighteous (1 Timothy 1:15).

Fifth, the effects of Law and Gospel are different. Walther summarizes the threefold effect of the Law: (1) It demands but does not enable compliance. (2) It hurls people into despair, for it diagnoses the disease but provides no cure. (3) It produces contrition, that is, it terrifies the conscience but offers no comfort. Walther echoes the early Lutheran hymn writer Paul Speratus, who captured the biblical teaching of the Law's lethal effectiveness:

> What God did in his Law demand
> And none to him could render
> Caused wrath and woe on ev'ry hand
> For man, the vile offender.
> Our flesh has not those pure desires
> The spirit of the Law requires,

And lost is our condition.

It was a false, misleading dream
That God his Law had given
That sinners could themselves redeem
And by their works gain heaven.
The Law is but a mirror bright
To bring the inbred sin to light
That lurks within our nature.[3]

Public debates have raged over whether or not the Ten Commandments should be displayed in courtrooms and classrooms. Sometimes well-meaning people have argued that placards containing the Ten Commandments would have a positive effect on public morality. Actually, the Scriptures teach that the Law makes matters worse, not better. Knowledge of the Law does not entail the ability to keep it. The Law not only identifies sin but also, like a swift kick to a sleeping dog that arouses the animal to bark and bite, the Law stirs up the power of sin (Romans 7:7–9). The Law brings death, not life, for it is a letter that kills (2 Corinthians 3:6). Without the Gospel, the Law can only be the cause for grief, as it was in the case of the rich young man who thought himself capable of keeping the Law (Matthew 19:22).

At each point, the Gospel is completely different from the Law. While it is only through faith that we receive the benefits of the Gospel, the Gospel itself creates faith (Romans 1:16; Ephesians 2:8–10). Rather than provoking terror of conscience, anguish of heart, and fear of condemnation like the Law, the Gospel stills every voice of accusation with the strong words of Christ's own peace and joy guaranteed by the blood of the cross. The Gospel does not set in place requirements of something that we must do or contribute. "[T]he Gospel does not require anything good that man must furnish: not a good heart, not a good disposition, no improvement of his condition, no godliness, no love either of God or men. It issues no orders, but changes man. It plants love into his heart and makes him capable of all good works. It demands nothing, but it gives all. Should not this fact make us leap for joy?" (Walther, 16).

Sixth, Law and Gospel are to be distinguished in relation to the persons who are addressed. "The Law is to be preached to secure sinners and the Gospel to alarmed sinners" (Walther, 17). The secure sinner is the person who glories in his own self-righteousness. In the words of Lutheran theologian Gerhard Forde, the secure sinner is "addicted either to what is base or to what is high, either to lawlessness or to lawfulness. Theologically there is not any difference since both break the relationship to God, the giver."[4] Addicted to that which is base, secure sinners will excuse or rationalize their sinful behavior. They will live, to use the words of the confessional prayer, "as if God did not matter and as if I mattered most."[5] They will assert that their body and life and that of their neighbors are theirs to do with as they please. Or secure sinners might be addicted to that which is high. Like the Pharisee in Jesus' parable (Luke 18:9–14), secure sinners will trust in their own righteousness, their self-made spirituality. The sinners who are snug in their own righteousness rehearse the Ten Commandments and conclude that they, like the rich young man in the Gospel narrative, have kept all of these rules and are deserving of God's approval. To those ensnared in either of these securities, blind to God's demand for total righteousness, the Law is to be proclaimed full blast so all presumption might be destroyed.

To those who have been crushed by the hammer blows of the Law, no longer secure in their lawlessness or self-righteousness, there is only one word that will do. That is the word of the Gospel. The Gospel is not a recipe for self-improvement. It is that word of God that declares sins to be forgiven for the sake of the suffering and death of Jesus Christ. It is all about Christ and what He has done for us. "Law is to be called, and to be, anything that refers to what we are to do. On the other hand, the Gospel, or the Creed, is any doctrine or word of God which does not require works from us and does not command us to do something, but bids us simply accept as a gift the gracious forgiveness of our sins and everlasting bliss offered us" (Walther, 19).

When Law and Gospel are muddled or mixed, the Holy Scriptures will be misread and misused. Without the right distinction of the Law from the Gospel, the Bible appears to be a book riddled with contradiction. At one place it condemns and at another it pardons. One text speaks of God's wrath visited upon sinners, while another declares His undying love for His enemies. Throughout both the Old and the New Testaments, the Scriptures reveal both God's wrath and His favor. The Scriptures show us a God who kills and who makes alive. This God does so through two different words. With the word of His Law, sinners are put to death. It is only through the word of the Gospel that spiritual corpses are resurrected to live in Jesus Christ. Unlike the Law, the Gospel speaks of Christ's own righteousness that comes not as our accomplishment but as His freely given gift received by faith. According to the Formula of Concord:

> The distinction between law and gospel is a particularly glorious light. It serves to divide God's Word properly (cf. 2 Tim. 2:15) and to explain correctly and make understandable the writings of the holy prophets and apostles. Therefore, we must diligently preserve this distinction, so as not to mix these two teachings together and make the gospel into a law. For this obscures the merit of Christ and robs troubled consciences of the comfort that they otherwise have in the holy gospel when it is preached clearly and purely. With the help of this distinction these consciences can sustain themselves in their greatest spiritual struggles against the terror of the law.[6]

Without this distinction, the radiance of the Scriptures is rendered dim, and we are left in doubt about God's mercy for sinners.

The Law tells us about ourselves. What it shows us is not good. It diagnoses the sickness of our sin and puts death before us. The Gospel, on the other hand, shows us the pure grace and favor of God in Jesus Christ. It shows us a God who is not against us but for us, even to the point of death on the cross.

For Reflection and Discussion

1. Read Romans 3:19–28. What does Paul tell us about the scope and purpose of the Law? What does Paul tell us about the scope and purpose of the Gospel?

2. How was the Law revealed? Where is the Gospel revealed?

3. How are the Law and Gospel different according to both content and effect?

4. Tolerance has become the chief and perhaps only virtue of the early years of the twenty-first century. How does uncritical tolerance confuse Law and Gospel?

5. Read Matthew 19:16–22. How did the rich young man misuse the Law? Was his problem lawlessness or lawfulness? How did Jesus use the Law to expose this man's sin?

6. Read 2 Timothy 2:15. How are the Scriptures misunderstood without the proper distinction of Law and Gospel? List contemporary examples of erroneous readings of the Bible that fail to distinguish Law and Gospel.

7. Reflect on these words from the Formula of Concord: "For since the proclamation of the law alone, without Christ, either makes presumptuous people, who believe that they can fulfill the law with their outward works, or drives people into total despair, Christ took the law into his own hands and interpreted it spiritually (Matt. 5:21–48 and Rom. 7:6–24). He thus revealed his 'wrath from heaven' upon all sinners and how great it is" (Solid Declaration V, 10 [K-W, 583]). Read Matthew 5:21–48 and Romans 7:6–24. How do these passages tell us about the scope and power of the Law?

Notes

1. James Arne Nestingen, "Distinguishing Law and Gospel: A Functional View" *Concordia Journal* 22 (January 1996): 27.

2. LW 31:231.

3. *Lutheran Worship* 355:2–3.

4. Gerhard Forde, *On Being a Theologian of the Cross* (Grand Rapids: Eerdmans, 1997), 27.

5. *Lutheran Worship*, p. 310.

6. Formula of Concord, Solid Declaration V, 1 (K-W, 581).

Chapter Two

THE HIGH AND HARD ART

> Only he is an orthodox teacher who not only presents all articles of faith in accordance with Scripture, but also rightly distinguishes from each other the Law and the Gospel.—C. F. W. Walther (Thesis II [Walther, 30])

> Rightly distinguishing the Law and the Gospel is the most difficult and the highest art of Christians in general and of theologians in particular. It is taught only by the Holy Spirit in the school of experience.—C. F. W. Walther (Thesis III [Walther, 42])

Teaching the Christian faith is more than repeating biblical words and phrases. It is an art that requires attention to the content and contours of the scriptural message, as well as the way that God's words do their work in exposing sin and bringing forgiveness to the repentant. Law-Gospel proclamation is reduced to generic slogans and empty assertions if attempted without the reliable content of the Holy Scriptures. Yet where proclamation is attempted without discerning the difference between the Law and the Gospel, the Scriptures are undercut, even if they are acknowledged as truthful.

Walther noted the corrosive acids of theological systems spawned by the Enlightenment that could not speak of Christian doctrine with any sense of certainty or finality. Truth was seen as elusive and beyond comprehension. Doctrine was defined as a human attempt to press the infinite into finite categories. Therefore, doctrine was thought to be in process and always under revision. The seeds that were sown by theologians of the Enlightenment are now being harvested in postmodern theologies that reject absolute truth altogether.

Confessional theology comes with a recognition that doctrine belongs to the Lord, but this is now being replaced by a variety of "constructive" theologies. Luther, in his 1535 lectures on Galatians, writes:

> Doctrine is heaven, life is earth. In life there is sin, error, uncleanness, and misery, mixed, as the saying goes, "with vinegar." Here love should condone, tolerate, be deceived, trust, hope, and endure all things (1 Cor. 13:7); here the forgiveness of sins should have complete sway, provided that sin and error are not defended. But just as there is no error in doctrine, so there is no need for any forgiveness of sins. Therefore there is no comparison at all between doctrine and life. "One dot" of doctrine is worth more than "heaven and earth" (Matt. 5:18); therefore we do not permit the slightest offense against it. But we can be lenient toward errors of life. For we, too, err daily in our life and conduct; so do all the saints, as they earnestly confess in the Lord's Prayer and the Creed. But by the grace of God our doctrine is pure; we have all the articles of faith solidly established in Sacred Scripture. The devil would dearly love to corrupt and overthrow these; that is why he attacks us so cleverly with this specious argument about not offending against love and the harmony among the churches.[1]

Doctrine is not from man but from God. It is not up for revision.

In an age of relativism and religious pluralism, it is essential to confess the full truth of God's Word. Nothing that our Lord gives us may be set aside. Any error diminishes the truth of the Gospel, making Christ less of a Savior than He is. Insistence on purity of doctrine is not a matter of rigidity or inflexibility but of faithfulness to our Lord. Yet Walther recognizes that a sermon may contain no false doctrine yet fail to preach Christ.

How can this be? Walther says:

> Only he is an orthodox teacher who, in addition to other requirements, rightly distinguishes Law and Gospel from each other. That is the final test of a proper sermon. The value of a sermon depends not only on this, that every statement in it be taken from the Word of God and be in agreement with the same, but also on this, whether Law and Gospel have been rightly divided. Of the same building materials furnished two architects one will construct a magnificent building, while the other, using the same materials, makes a botch of it. Crack-brained man that he is, he may want to begin at the roof or place all the windows in one room or pile up layers of stone or brick in such a fashion that a crooked wall will be the result. The one house will be out of plumb and such a bungling piece of work that it will collapse while the other stands firm and is a habitable and pleasant abode. In like manner all doctrines may be treated in sermons by two preachers: the one sermon may be a glorious and precious piece of work, while the other is wrong throughout. Note this well. When you hear some sectarian preach, you may say, "What he said was the truth," and yet you do not feel satisfied. Here is the key for unlocking this mystery: the preacher did not rightly divide Law and Gospel, and hence everything went wrong. (Walther, 32)

The content of the preaching may be correct in that it uses words from the Bible. The preacher does not deny the truthfulness of scriptural claims. Nonetheless, the sermon fails as evangelical preaching in this regard: The Law is presented as good news, or the Gospel is presented as something that we do. Such preaching, regardless of how many Bible passages are quoted or referenced, is not the preaching of Christ crucified as the only Savior of sinners. Luther says:

> It is therefore a matter of utmost necessity that these two kinds of God's Word be well and properly distinguished.

Where this is not done, neither the Law nor the Gospel can be understood, and the consciences of men must perish with blindness and error. The Law has its goal fixed beyond which it cannot go or accomplish anything, namely, until the point is reached where Christ comes in. It must terrify the impenitent with threats of the wrath and displeasure of God. Likewise the Gospel has its peculiar function and task, *viz.*, to proclaim forgiveness of sin to sorrowing souls. These may not be commingled, nor the one substituted for the other, without a falsification of doctrine. For while the Law and the Gospel are indeed equally God's Word, they are not the same doctrine. (Walther, 35)

"Do your best to present yourself to God as one approved, a worker who has no need to be ashamed, rightly handling the word of truth," says Paul (2 Timothy 2:15). In this epistle of pastoral instruction to Timothy, the seasoned apostle gets to the heart of the high art of the preacher's craft. Words of God are not thrown together like so many vegetables in a stew. To use Walther's illustration from carpentry, the builder does not join board to beam willy-nilly. Each element of a building is fitted together in such a way that a house results, not a pile of rubble. A pharmacist dispenses medicine according to the disease of the patient. Good medicine improperly administered can be fatal. Even so, pastors who are builders of God's house and physicians of the souls entrusted to their care are to be skilled in making the distinction between Law and Gospel.

This is no easy task. Like any art, it is not learned quickly or without ongoing practice. Luther calls it the highest art: "Distinguishing between the Law and the Gospel is the highest art in Christendom, one that every person who values the name Christian ought to recognize, know, and possess. Where this is lacking, it is not possible to tell who is Christian and who is pagan or Jew. That much is at stake in this distinction."[2]

Discerning Law from Gospel is not as easy as it first appears. Making the distinction requires more than a superficial look at the text. The real difficulty comes when the Law attacks the tender and terrified conscience, pressing to the point of despair even in the face of the promises of the Gospel. Walther describes it as a battle:

> Like two hostile forces, Law and Gospel sometimes clash with each other in a person's conscience. The Gospel says to him: "You have been received into God's grace." The Law says to him: "Do not believe it; for look at your past life. How many and grievous are your sins! Examine the thoughts and desires that you have harbored in your mind." On an occasion like this it is difficult to divide Law and Gospel. When this happens to a person, he must say to the Law: "Away with you! Your demands have all been fully met, and you have nothing to demand of me. There is One who has paid my debt." This difficulty does not occur to a person dead in his trespasses and sins; he is soon through with the Law. But the difficulty is quite real to a person who has been converted. (Walther, 47)

Luther makes a similar point in a letter to a young man vexed by Satan's attack and tempted to despair:

> When the devil attacks and torments us, we must completely set aside the whole Decalogue. When the devil throws our sins up to us and declares that we deserve death and hell, we ought to speak thus: "I admit that I deserve death and hell. What of it? Does this mean that I shall be sentenced to eternal damnation? By no means. For I know One who suffered and made satisfaction in my behalf. His name is Jesus Christ, the Son of God. Where he is, there I shall be also."[3]

When the conscience is under attack, one must abandon the Law completely. As the Law makes its move to accuse, driving to introspection and accusation, it offers no relief. God spoke to Israel in cloudy majesty and smoky awe from Mount Sinai's heights (see Exodus 19:16–25), giving them the Law. Sinai's Law unerringly sniffs out every scent of sin, uncovering our failure to fear, love, and trust in God above all things. It unmasks all pious pretensions. Sinai is deadly; there is no life on its peaks. There are no crevices in that mountain that will hide us from the Judge of all. There are no caves deep enough to shelter us from God's wrath. There is no consolation from Mount Sinai.

The Book of Hebrews tells us of another mountain: "But you have come to Mount Zion and to the city of the living God, the heavenly Jerusalem, and to innumerable angels in festal gathering, and to the assembly of the firstborn who are enrolled in heaven, and to God, the judge of all, and to the spirits of the righteous made perfect, and to Jesus, the mediator of a new covenant, and to the sprinkled blood that speaks a better word than the blood of Abel" (Hebrews 12:22–24).

The clash between Law and Gospel puts faith itself on trial. Is the Gospel really God's last and final word that trumps the accusation of the Law? Or is there something yet that I must do if I am to have peace with God? The ability to distinguish Law and Gospel is brought to the test when the heart condemns and accuses with the memory of past sins. Where does the tormented soul look? When we are crushed by Law, the only place we can find relief is in the wounds of Christ Jesus and the promise that His blood cleanses from all sin. This point is wonderfully illustrated in the novel *The Hammer of God* by the Swedish bishop Bo Giertz. In this story, Frans, a man known for his piety, lies dying. As often happens with a person on the edge of death, Frans's mind wanders back to the days before his conversion. Drifting in deliriousness, the dying man utters words of an oath and froths on about drinking and a fellow who had cheated him. Disturbed by the impious ramblings of her father, Lena exclaims, "You are thinking about Jesus, are you not, Father?" Frans replies, "I am not able to, Lena. I can't think any longer. But I know that Jesus is thinking about me."[4] With those words, a dying man distinguishes Law from Gospel and dies a Christian death. The Gospel is not about our ability to think of Christ but about His promise as the friend of sinners, His promise that nothing will pluck us from His hands (John 10:28).

For Reflection and Discussion

1. What makes the proper distinction of Law from Gospel such a difficult art?

2. Why does Luther exalt doctrine over life? Many in our day are opposed to dogma. The slogan "Deeds, not creeds" is a popular way to make light of biblical teaching. How does this slogan confuse Law and Gospel?

3. Why does Luther counsel the person tormented by his sin "to set aside the whole Decalogue"?

4. How does the clash between Law and Gospel put faith itself on trial? See 1 John 3:19–23.

5. Read Hebrews 12:18–24. How does Mount Sinai (see Exodus 19:16–25) embody the Law? How does Hebrews picture Mount Zion as the place of the Gospel?

6. How does the story of Frans in *The Hammer of God* illustrate the comfort of the Gospel?

7. Proclaiming Law and Gospel is much more difficult than measuring up eight ounces of Law and ten ounces of Gospel. How does a pastor become a craftsman who handles God's Word correctly, rightly distinguishing Law and Gospel? How does a Christian know when to speak Law and when to speak Gospel in witness to an unbeliever?

Notes

1. LW 27:41–42.

2. Martin Luther, "The Distinction between Law and Gospel: A Sermon by Martin Luther," trans. Willard L. Burce, *Concordia Journal* 18 (April 1992): 154. Also see appendix.

3. Theodore Tappert, comp., *Luther: Letters of Spiritual Counsel* (Louisville: Westminster/John Knox, 1955), 86–87.

4. Bo Giertz, *The Hammer of God*, trans. Clifford A. Nelson (Minneapolis: Augsburg, 1973), 193–94.

Chapter Three

MAKING CHRIST A NEW MOSES

The first manner of confounding Law and Gospel is the one most easily recognized—and the grossest. It is adopted, for instance, by the Papists, Socinians, and the Rationalists and consists in this, that Christ is represented as a new Moses, or Lawgiver, and the Gospel turned into a doctrine of meritorious works, while at the same time those who teach that the Gospel is the message of the free grace of God in Christ are condemned and anathematized, as is done by the papists.— C. F. W. Walther (Thesis V [Walther, 69])

When human works are added to the Gospel, the Gospel ceases to be good news about Christ. Walther goes to the Council of Trent—the Roman Catholic response to the Reformation—for a prime example of this confusion of Law and Gospel. The Council of Trent assembled in 1545 and met (with two interruptions, one of three and one of ten years) through 1563. Convened to provide a definitive condemnation of the Reformation and to set in place reforms to counteract its influence, the council rejected the Lutheran teaching that justification is by faith alone. In explaining his fifth thesis, Walther takes aim at Trent's assertion that the Gospel is not only "the source of all saving truth" but also a "*moral norm*" (Walther, 69, *Walther's emphasis*).

This false teaching is not limited to the Church of Rome. Walther mentions Socinians and Rationalists. The Socinians were an anti-trinitarian group active in Italy at the time of the Reformation. Because they denied the deity of Christ and His atonement, they could only teach a Christ who was a model for godly living. Later, Rationalism would attempt to strip Christianity of its supernatural and sacramental character, leaving only a Christ who stood as the highest pinnacle in the evolution of morality. Rationalism saw Christ as the embodiment of the ethical life. Christianity in this scheme consisted of following His example in charitable living. In short order it developed into mere humanism disguised under a thin veneer of Bible verses.

Walther will not have the streams of living waters polluted with the toxic waste of self-made righteousness. Again quoting the documents of the Council of Trent, he declares:

> In Canon 21, adopted at its sixth session, the synagog of Satan decrees: "If any one says that Christ Jesus has been given by God to men that He should be their Redeemer, in whom they are to trust, and not also their Lawgiver, whom they are to obey, let him be anathema." This decree overthrows the Christian religion completely. If Christ came into the world to publish new laws to us, we should feel like saying that He might as well have stayed in heaven. Moses had already given us so perfect a Law that we could not fulfil it. Now, if Christ had given us additional laws, that would have had to drive to despair. (Walther, 70)

Ecumenically sensitive ears that are no longer attuned to the critical necessity for the right distinction of Law and Gospel will be offended at the harshness of Walther's language. Yet Walther's polemic is derived from his passion for the proclamation of the pure Gospel to hurting sinners. Broken sinners do not need instructions in ethics but a word from God that rescues them from the misery of their sin and restores them to peace with God through faith in His promises.

In a morally decadent culture, there is a temptation to make

Jesus a new Moses. Amid the chaos of a world that recognizes no absolutes, should not the church proclaim biblical morality? Yes, the church must proclaim God's Law. The Law of God orders and curbs our sinful impulses, keeping life genuinely human in this world. More than that, the Law unerringly exposes the darkness of our unbelief, our failure to fear, love, and trust in God above all things. This Law is also needed in the life of the Christian, for the Christian continues in this life as both "saint and sinner"—both old and new man in one body. But the Gospel contains not an ounce of Law.

Jesus does not come as the giver of moral norms. Moses does that needed work. Jesus comes as the friend of sinners. He comes as the Savior from the condemnation that the Law pronounces and delivers. The apostle Paul writes of this in Galatians: "But when the fullness of time had come, God sent forth His Son, born of woman, born under the law, to redeem those who were under the law, so that we might receive adoption as sons" (Galatians 4:4–5). The sinless Son of God comes to take our sin on Himself and to suffer under its penalty on the cross that we might have His righteousness not by imitation but by faith alone.

The false teaching of the Council of Trent is with us still. Roman Catholics remain unwilling to confess that salvation is by faith alone. On Reformation Day 1999, representatives of the Roman Catholic Church and the Lutheran World Federation joined in a festive worship service around the signing of the *Joint Declaration on the Doctrine of Justification*. Sadly, this much celebrated document failed to resolve the real issue at stake in the Reformation debate, namely, the question of whether God's justification of the ungodly is by faith alone or whether human works of love have a part to play in salvation. The decrees of the Council of Trent have not been revoked.[1] Rome still sees justification as a process that is happening in man as he is transformed by the grace of God. Confessional Lutherans confess that justification is solely the work of Jesus Christ. But the problem resides not only in Rome. We see in other ways that the Gospel is misspoken as well. What message do the popular "WWJD?" (What Would Jesus Do?) bracelets convey? Do they not give the picture that the main thing about being a Christian is conforming oneself to the model of Jesus?

Luther noted that Christ is a gift before He is an example:

> Be sure, moreover, that you do not make Christ into a Moses, as if Christ did nothing more than teach and provide examples as the other saints do, as if the gospel were simply a textbook of teachings or laws. Therefore you should grasp Christ, his words, works, and sufferings, in a twofold manner. First as an example that is presented to you, which you should follow and imitate. As St. Peter says in 1 Peter 4, "Christ suffered for us, thereby leaving us an example." Thus when you see how he prays, fasts, helps people, and shows them love, so also you should do, both for yourself and your neighbor. However this is the smallest part of the gospel, on the basis of which it cannot yet even be called gospel. For on this level Christ is of no more help to you than some other saint. His life remains His own and does not as yet contribute anything to you. In short this mode (of understanding Christ as simply an example) does not make Christians but only hypocrites. You must grasp Christ at a much higher level. Even though this higher level has for a long time been the very best, the preaching of it has become rare. The chief article and foundation of the gospel is that before you take Christ as an example, you accept and recognize him as a gift, as a present that God has given you and that is your own. This means that when you see or hear of Christ doing or suffering something, you do not doubt that Christ himself, with his deeds and suffering, belongs to you.[2]

Christ as example still leaves us under the Law. Luther quips that if salvation were dependent on following Jesus' example, we would all be doomed from the start, for who of us has been born of a virgin or walks on water? There is no salvation in Christ as our example, for none of us can live the perfect and sinless life that He lived.

Both the Old and New Testament proclaim the God who graciously comes to sinners to save them. Walther says:

> Any one, therefore, imagining that Christ is a new Lawgiver and has brought us new laws cancels the entire Christian religion. For he removes that by which the Christian religion differs from all other religions in the world. All other religions say to man: "You must become just so and so and do such works if you wish to go to heaven." Over against this the Christian religion says: "You are a lost and condemned sinner; you cannot be your own Savior. But do not despair on that account. There is One who has acquired salvation for you. Christ has opened the portals of heaven to you and says to you: Come, for all things are ready. Come to the marriage of the Lamb." That is the reason, too, why Christ says: "I heal the sick, not them that are whole. I am come to seek and save that which was lost. I am not come to call the righteous, but sinners, to repentance." (Walther, 71–72)

Adolph Köberle observes that apart from the Gospel, human beings will seek access to God by moralism, rationalism, or mysticism.[3] Moralism seeks access to God on the presupposition that our good works must advance our standing before God. Rationalism elevates human reason, confusing human wisdom with God's revelation. Mysticism seeks immediate union with God through emotional experience. Moralism, rationalism, and mysticism represent strivings for God fueled by the Law. Without the true God, man will always attempt to create a substitute deity. Luther captures this reality in the Large Catechism:

> Look, here you have the true honor and worship that please God, which God also commands under penalty of eternal wrath, namely, that the heart should know no other consolation or confidence than in him, nor let itself be torn from him, but for his sake should risk everything and disregard everything else on earth. On the other hand, you will easily see and judge how the world practices nothing but false worship and idolatry. There has never been a nation so

wicked that it did not establish and maintain some sort of worship. All people have set up their own god, to whom they looked for blessings, help, and comfort.[4]

The problem is not so much atheism as it is idolatry. The idols that human beings construct are poor replacements for the true and living God.

The God of the Scriptures is not a deity created by human imagination. His ways are not our ways (see Isaiah 55:8). He has made foolish the wisdom of this world (see 1 Corinthians 1:20). God operates in a way that confounds all man-made religious systems and self-styled spirituality. The wisdom of the old Adam consistently attempts to approach God on the basis of the Law. This is true of the old Adam as he traffics in the terrain of good works, rational thinking, or emotional experience. Yet the Law shuts down every highway we construct to reach God. The Law posts a "No Exit" sign over every doorway we go through to try and meet God on our own terms. The Gospel stands in contrast to all religions of the Law, for it does not invite us to become righteous on the basis of our own morality, reason, or emotion. It announces a God who comes to seek out the lost and receive sinners into His fellowship (see 1 Timothy 1:15). The Gospel proclaims a God who sent His Son into the world not to condemn the world but to rescue the world by His death on the cross (John 3:17). It is this Gospel and not the Law that is "the power of God for salvation to everyone who believes" (Romans 1:16).

Commandments have their place, but not in the Gospel. When it comes to salvation, the Gospel is exclusive. It excludes all human works from salvation—even the works that are wrought in us by the Holy Spirit. These good works are not the root but the fruit of faith. Walther observes:

> In its sixth session the Council of Trent passed this decree: "If any one says that men are made righteous solely through the imputation of the righteousness of Christ or solely through the forgiveness of sin, to the exclusion of the grace and love which by the Holy Spirit is poured out in

their hearts and is inherent in them; or that the grace by which we are made righteous is nothing else than the favor of God,—let him be accursed. If any one says that the faith which makes men righteous is nothing else than trust in the divine mercy, which remits sins for Christ's sake, or that it is only this trust that makes us righteous,—let him be accursed. . . . If any one says that a justified person does not, by reason of the good *works* which are done by him through the grace of God and the merit of Jesus Christ, whose living member he is, truly *merit* an increase of grace, eternal life, and the actual obtainment of eternal life, provided he dies in grace—let him be accursed." (Walther, 74, *Walther's emphasis*)

The decrees of the Council of Trent remain official teaching in the Roman Catholic Church.

The Gospel does not burden stricken consciences with demands for moral living. It simply offers rest from the demands of the Law. It gives this rest in Christ who has fulfilled the Law for us. In excluding all good works, the Gospel actually enlivens the Christian to live a life of good works that spring not from the compulsion of the Law but, as the Formula of Concord puts it, "from a free and merry spirit."[5] Removed from the Gospel, good works are relocated where they belong: in the world, as they glorify God and serve the neighbor in his or her need.

FOR REFLECTION AND DISCUSSION

1. Read Galatians 1:6–9. Why does Paul place those who preach a "different gospel" under a curse? How does this help us understand Walther's condemnation of the Council of Trent? There is an axiom of long-standing in the church that declares "the church that cannot curse can no longer bless." In our tolerant age, many find it hard to reject false teaching. Why is this so?

2. Why does Luther insist that Christ is a gift before He is an example? When Christ is pictured merely as an example or model for Christian living, what happens to the Gospel? What evidence can you find of this confusion in contemporary Christianity?

3. How are rationalism, moralism, and mysticism dead-end paths to God?

4. What do each of these texts tell us about the Gospel? 1 Timothy 1:17; John 3:17; 1 Corinthians 1:18–25; and Romans 1:16.

5. Writing on "the righteousness of the new obedience," that is, the life that springs from the righteousness of faith, the Formula of Concord says: "For because this righteousness (of the new obedience) that is begun in us—this renewal—is imperfect and impure in this life because of our flesh, a person cannot use it in any way to stand before God's judgment throne. Instead, only the righteousness of the obedience, suffering, and death of Christ, which is reckoned to faith, can stand before God's tribunal. Even following their renewal, when they are already producing many good works and living the best kind of life, human beings please God, are acceptable to him, and receive adoption as children and heirs of eternal life only because of Christ's obedience" (Solid Declaration III, 32 [K-W, 567–68]). In light of these words, how are we to understand the place of good works in the life of the Christian?

NOTES

1. See Robert Preus, *Justification and Rome* (St. Louis: Concordia Academic Press, 1997), 103–15.

2. LW 35:119.

3. Adolph Köberle, *The Quest for Holiness*, trans. John Mattes (Minneapolis: Augsburg, 1936), 1–18.

4. Large Catechism, "The Ten Commandments," 16–17 (K-W, 388).

5. Formula of Concord, Solid Declaration VI, 17 (K-W, 590).

Chapter Four

THE MIX MAKES THE MUDDLE

In the second place, the Word of God is not rightly divided when the Law is not preached in its full sternness and the Gospel not in its full sweetness, when, on the contrary, Gospel elements are mingled with the Law and Law elements with the Gospel.—C. F. W. Walther (Thesis VI [Walther, 79])

To bring the Law into the domain of the Gospel is to undermine the good news of Jesus Christ, transforming a pure gift into a human achievement. Such mingling of Law with Gospel dilutes the precious promises of God with demands for works. In short, the Gospel is polluted and rendered impotent. To use another biblical metaphor, a pinch of the yeast of the Law hidden away in the dough of the Gospel ruins the whole lump. We are not left with the bread of life but with stale rations that cannot sustain those who journey through the valley of death's shadow.

On the other hand, to mix the Gospel into the Law is to create the illusion that the Law offers hope. Inserted into the Law, the Gospel weakens but does not remove the threat of the Law. Such a blending of Law and Gospel invites sinners to place their confidence in their own efforts—"motivated by the Gospel," as it is said. The Law is lifted up as a set of principles or rules that may be obeyed and fulfilled with the aid of God's grace. This synthesis of Law and Gospel corrupts both, driving broken sinners either to a false security or to unholy despair.

In his defense of Thesis VI, Walther turns to Galatians 3:11–12 where the apostle Paul says: "Now it is evident that no one is justified before God by the law, for 'The righteous shall live by faith.' But the law is not of faith, rather 'The one who does them shall live by them.' " The Law has absolutely no power to make human beings righteous. It has nothing to say about God's grace in Jesus Christ. It cannot create faith. The faith that the Law demands is not a work that we can accomplish. Faith is purely passive, completely receptive of the gift of forgiveness bestowed by the Gospel alone. "For when God creates faith in man, this is as great a work as if He were to create heaven and earth again," says Luther.[1] This faith comes by hearing the Gospel, not the Law. "So faith comes from hearing, and hearing through the word of Christ" (Romans 10:17). The Law creates the knowledge of sin, but it is powerless to give the knowledge of salvation (Romans 3:20).

There is no sweetness in the Law. Walther warns against every attempt to take the edge off the Law by making it less lethal than it is. He says:

> No Gospel element, then, must be mingled with the Law. Any one expounding the Law shamefully perverts it by injecting into it grace, the grace, loving-kindness, and patience of God, who forgives sin. He acts like a sick-nurse, who fetches sugar to sweeten the bitter medicine, which the patient dislikes. What is the result? Why, the medicine does not take effect, and the patient remains feverish. In order that it might retain its strength the medicine should not have been sweetened. A preacher must proclaim the Law in such a manner that there remains in it nothing pleasant to lost and condemned sinners. Every sweet ingredient injected into the Law is poison; it renders this heavenly medicine ineffective, neutralizes its operation. (Walther, 80)

The Law remains Law and the Gospel remains Gospel. Jesus did not come to destroy or displace the Law but to fulfill it (see Matthew 5:17–19). So in proclaiming the Law, its threats must be spoken without adulteration. "When preaching the Law, you must ever bear in mind that the Law makes no concessions. That is utterly beside the character of the Law; it only makes demands" (Walther, 80).

God gave humankind His holy Law imprinted on the heart and inscribed on tablets of stone at Sinai. He gave the Ten Commandments, not the "ten suggestions," as one wag put it. God's Law is not an arbitrary imposition on human beings. It is a divine requirement that imposes itself "out of the conditions of creaturely life,"[2] to borrow a phrase from James Nestingen. It will not relax its limits. The Law cannot be toned down as though God were not absolutely serious in His demands for perfection. It is impossible to whittle the Law down to manageable size as though the Almighty, like a doting schoolteacher, might grade on a curve, relaxing His stringent standards.

The Law strikes no bargains with sinners; it only condemns. The old Adam is tempted to use the Law to save himself. Adding even the slightest element of the Gospel to the Law encourages his inborn legalism, the thought that he has something to contribute to his standing before God. Bo Giertz exposes this temptation through a conversation between Pastor Torvik and a wise, elderly woman, Mother Lotta, in his novel *The Hammer of God*. Pastor Torvik has completely confused Law and Gospel in his zealous efforts to make his parishioners "better Christians." Mother Lotta reminds her pastor that "it won't do to offer Moses a forty percent agreement and expect him to be satisfied with our becoming absolutely pure and loving and honest, as you are always talking about."[3] Mother Lotta knew more about the art of distinguishing Law and Gospel than did the novice pastor. There is no hope in the Law. The Law will not settle for our best efforts or our good intentions. It demands perfection and nothing less.

God's Law goes to the heart. It has as its target not only outward performance but also inward fear, love, and trust in God above all things. The Law is not a club to beat the mischievous into submission. Yes, it does "curb" the external vices of sinners, holding them in check and preserving some order in this chaotic world until the Lord Christ returns to expel sin forever. But that is not all it does. God's Law is a sharp sword that slices away all the flimsy excuses we use to cover our shame and defend ourselves against God. It is a saber that puts to death.

Walther warns young preachers not to confuse genuine preaching of the Law with jeremiads against evil.

> A sermon on the Law which you deliver from your pulpit, to be a proper preaching of the Law, must measure up to these requirements: There is to be no ranting about the abominable vices that may be rampant in the congregation. Continual ranting will prove useless. People may quit the practises that have been reproved, but in two weeks they will have relapsed into their old ways. You must, indeed, testify with great earnestness against transgressions of God's commandments, but you must also tell the people: "Even if you were to quit your habitual cursing, swearing, and the like, that would not make you Christians. You might go to perdition for all that. God is concerned about the attitude of your heart." (Walther, 81)

In our day, some confuse the proper preaching of the Law with condemnation of outbreaks of immorality such as abortion or homosexuality. The danger in such preaching is that those who are not homosexuals or who have never procured or supported abortion conclude that they have fulfilled the Law. Such preaching creates smug Pharisees rather than repentant tax collectors. While homosexuality and abortion are surely sinful and as such fall under the condemnation of God's Law, the Law itself digs deeper. The Law with laser-like precision penetrates to the heart. Jesus' preaching demonstrates genuine proclamation of the Law. When Jesus preached His Sermon on Mount, He was preaching to a congregation that knew the Ten Commandments. They understood that Moses prohibited adultery and that the Fifth Commandment outlawed murder. Jesus plunges the dagger of the Law into the heart: "You have heard that it was said to those of old, 'You shall not murder; and whoever murders will be liable to judgment.' But I say to you that everyone who is angry with his brother will be liable to judgment. . . . You have heard that it was said, 'You shall not commit adultery.' But I say to you that everyone who looks at a woman with lustful intent has already committed adultery with her in his heart" (Matthew 5:21–22, 27–28). The Law drives a dagger to the heart. Where the Law is seen only as regulating external actions, commanding what we are to do and not to do, it has not yet reached its God-given goal. When the Law is not preached in such a way as to uncover unbelief, it will create Pharisees. Morality will be confused with faith. And the Law itself will be heard as good news.

Every attempt to diminish the Law is bound to confuse Law and Gospel. Prior to the Reformation, the Roman Church attempted to make the Law more doable by defining some of Jesus' teachings as "evangelical counsels." These "hard sayings" of the Lord that required poverty, chastity of mind and body, suffering without retaliation, and so forth were seen as prescriptions only for the spiritually elite (monks and nuns). These teachings were beyond the grasp of ordinary Christians. God's Law may not be interpreted so as to justify those who break it. The Law offers no way of escape. As Paul says: "Now we know that whatever the law says it speaks to those who are under the law, so that every mouth may be stopped, and the whole world may be held accountable to God. For by the works of the law no human being will be justified in His sight, since through the law comes knowledge of sin" (Romans 3:19–20).

The Law never finds righteousness; it only confirms unrighteousness. The Gospel never finds righteousness; it only gives and bestows righteousness. The righteousness imparted by the Gospel is not one of works but of God's grace in the blood of Jesus Christ. It is a righteousness that is not achieved but received by faith alone. Luther's penitential hymn gets it right:

> Your grace and love alone avail
> To blot out my sin with pardon.
> In your gaze our best efforts pale,
> Develop pride, and harden.
> Before your throne no one can boast
> That he escaped sin's deadly coast.
> Our haven is your mercy.
>
> In God, I anchor all my trust,
> Discarding my own merit.
> His love holds firm; I therefore must
> His fullest grace inherit.
> He tells me, and my heart has heard
> The steadfast promise of his Word,
> That he's my help and haven.[4]

Unrelenting in its demand, the Law can only make sin manifest for what it is and crush the sinner with its death sentence. There is no way to soften the hammer blows of the Law with promises of goodness to those who keep it or who at least attempt to live by its dictates. The Law remains a word from the Lord that unmasks sin and accuses the sinner. It is to be preached in its full sternness, demonstrating that no one has "escaped sin's deadly coast." It is only when a person sees himself to be a genuine sinner with no hope under the Law that the Gospel will be heard as joyous news of pardon. Then the Gospel can be preached fully and freely, without any additives from the Law, as a word that makes no demands, invites no bartering, but simply declares the forgiveness of sins to lost and condemned creatures, flesh and blood sinners. The Gospel has nothing to do with our works or worthiness and everything to do with God's Son, Jesus Christ, who was put to death for our sins and raised again for our justification. "What law requires is freedom from the law,"[5] said the Danish theologian Leif Grane. This freedom is found only in the Law-free Gospel of Jesus Christ (Galatians 5:1).

For Reflection and Discussion

1. How does the synthesis of Law and Gospel undermine both of these words of God? Reflect on these words from Luther:

   "I say that, if we are ever to stand before God with a right and uncolored faith, we must come to the point where we learn clearly to distinguish and separate between ourselves, our life, and Christ the mercy seat. But he who will not do this, but immediately runs headlong to the judgment seat, will find it all right and get a good knock on the head. I have been there myself and was so burnt that I was glad I was able to come to the mercy seat. And now I am compelled to say: Even though I may have lived a good life before men, let everything I have done or failed to do remain there under the judgment seat as God sees fit, but, as for me, I know of no other comfort, help, or counsel for my salvation except that Christ is my mercy seat, who did no sin or evil and both died and rose again for me, and now sits at the right hand of the Father and takes me under his shadow and protection, so that I need have no doubt that through him I am safe before God from all wrath and terror. Thus faith remains pure and unalloyed, because then it makes no pretensions and seeks no glory or comfort save in the Lord Christ alone." (LW 51:282)

2. Read Galatians 3:1–14. How had the Galatians mingled the Law with the Gospel? How does the apostle Paul demonstrate that faith is not a work of the Law in this text?

3. Analyze this statement: "The Gospel demands that we show love to our neighbor in need." How does it confuse Law with Gospel?

4. A pastor urges his congregation to "do the Gospel" by launching an aggressive program of evangelism in the community. On the basis of Thesis VI, how might Walther respond to such an appeal? Troubled at the prospect of "cheap grace" and moral laxity, some Christians have urged that "we need to put some teeth into the Gospel." How does such an admonition diminish the Gospel?

5. Reflect on these words from a sermon by Luther in 1532: "For the Law has its terminus, defining how far it is to go and what it is to

achieve, namely, to terrify the impenitent with the wrath and displeasure of God and drive them to Christ. Likewise the Gospel has its unique office and function: to preach the forgiveness of sins to the troubled consciences. Let the doctrine then not be falsified, either by mingling these two into one, or by mistaking the one for the other" (Martin Luther, "The Distinction between Law and Gospel: A Sermon by Martin Luther," trans. Willard L. Burce, *Concordia Journal* 18 [April 1992]: 154). What are the limits of the Law? What is the "unique office and function" of the Gospel?

NOTES

1. LW 30:14.

2. James Arne Nestingen, "The Lord's Prayer in Luther's Catechisms," *Word & World* 22 (Winter 2002): 39.

3. Bo Giertz, *The Hammer of God*, trans. Clifford A. Nelson (Minneapolis: Augsburg, 1973), 281–82.

4. *Lutheran Worship* 230:2–3.

5. Gerhard Forde, *On Being a Theologian of the Cross* (Grand Rapids: Eerdmans, 1997), 29.

Chapter Five

FIRST THINGS FIRST

In the third place, the Word of God is not rightly divided when the Gospel is preached first and then the Law; sanctification first and then justification; faith first and then repentance; good works first and then grace.—C. F. W. Walther (Thesis VII [Walther, 89])

In the fourth place, the Word of God is not rightly divided when the Law is preached to those who are already in terror on account of their sins or the Gospel to those who live securely in their sins.—C. F. W. Walther (Thesis VIII [Walther, 101])

Without the prior work of the Law, the Gospel itself is perverted as it is reduced to nice words about God with sentimental appeal but completely void of the forgiveness of sins. "We live in an age," says Alan Jones, "in which everything is permitted and nothing is forgiven."[1] This makes the right use of Law and Gospel all the more pressing. First things must be kept first. The Law comes before the Gospel, justification before sanctification, repentance before faith, and grace before good works.

Walther begins his discussion of Thesis VII by asserting the priority of the Law in proclamation. The Good News will not be heard in all of its goodness if the Law has not been spoken. While this may appear self-evident, the history of the church bears sad witness to cases where the Gospel was preached before or without the Law. One such case was that of John Agricola (1492?–1566) at the time of the Reformation. Agricola studied at Wittenberg, where he came to know Luther and embraced his theology. However, later in his life, Agricola departed from Luther's understanding of Law and Gospel, claiming that true repentance is not the result of the Law but flows from the sweetness of the Gospel. Agricola asserted that the Law belongs in the courtroom, not the church. Hence, his position was identified as "antinomianism." Luther responded to this confusion of Law and Gospel with an open letter entitled "Against the Antinomians" in 1539. In this tract, Luther says:

> Preach that sinners must be roused to repentance not only by the sweet grace and suffering of Christ, by the message that he died for us, but also by the terrors of the law .... For who could know what and why Christ suffered for us without knowing what sin or the law is? Therefore the law must be preached wherever Christ is to be preached, even if the word "law" is not mentioned, so that the conscience is nevertheless frightened by the law when it hears that Christ had to fulfill the law for us at so great a price. Why, then, should one wish to abolish the law, which cannot be abolished, yes, which is only intensified by such an attempt? For the law terrifies me more ... than it would were it preached without the mention of Christ and such great torment suffered by God's Son, but were accompanied only by threats.[2]

Only where the Law has crushed sinners does the Gospel do its gracious work of healing the broken-hearted. The Law must kill the old Adam if the Gospel is to resurrect a new man to walk before God in righteousness and holiness. The Law cannot be reasoned away by theological sleight of hand. That is why Gerhard Forde calls antinomianism a "fake theology." It is a fake theology, "for if you want to remove the law, it is necessary to remove sin and death,"[3] says Luther. Only Christ can to that! When antinomians ancient or modern try to make the Law go away by theological quackery, they only succeed in relocating the Law. They end up inserting it into the Gospel. That makes for a legalized Gospel, which is no comfort to sinners. It only encourages them to live in the fantasy that sin is not so lethal after all.

Mark Twain once said, "Wagner's music is not as bad as it sounds." Some folks think of sin like that: "It is not as bad as it sounds." God's Law shows us how bad sin really is. Witness the preaching of John the Baptist in Matthew 3:1–12. This strange figure, more at home in the Judean wilderness than in Jerusalem's temple, would not let his congregation escape the reality of sin. Outfitted in garments of camel hair and feasting on a diet of locusts and honey, John will not leave us alone to bury our sins under psychological explanations or sociological observations. He will not listen to our protests that we are hapless victims of the evil of others. John does not relent. He calls us to repentance, to the confession that we are actually guilty, that we are nothing other than sinners who stand accountable to the living God for the mess we have made of our lives. It is as bad as it sounds. Sin really is an offense to God and it puts us under His wrath. The preaching of John the Baptist makes it clear that sinners are on the endangered species list.

John's preaching singled out the Pharisees and the Sadducees. These were the decent people of Jerusalem. They were not the murderers and adulterers, the boozers and embezzlers; these were the respectable people who worshiped in the temple and gave their tithes. John the Baptist called these spiritually elite men a brood of vipers. They were snakes worthy of God's wrath, not to be protected by a retreat to their pedigree as sons of Abraham. The Law that John preaches slices through our outward veneer, no matter how thick or thin, and leaves bare the heart. The heart unveiled by the Law is no valentine. "The heart is deceitful above all things, and desperately sick; who can understand it?" asks the prophet Jeremiah (Jeremiah 17:9).

The Law finds hearts made hard by unbelief and, therefore, barren of the fruits of faith. These are trees good only to be cut down. As a pine has no defense against the lumberman's ax, sinners have no defense against God's wrath. It is as bad as it sounds, for we have sinned against God in thought, word, and deed. These are not words mindlessly mouthed from Sunday to Sunday. They are words that accurately describe our lost condition. We must say with David: "For I know my transgressions, and my sin is ever before me. Against You, You only, have I sinned and done what is evil in Your sight, so that You may be justified in Your words and blameless in Your judgment" (Psalm 51:3–5).

John the Baptist takes from us every straw we grasp in a vain attempt to defend ourselves against God. He blocks every route we take to run away from God. There is finally no escaping Him; we will meet Him either in wrath or mercy. It is John's proper task to prepare us to meet our God in His mercy. Luther describes the work of John as a preacher of repentance:

> This is really what it means to begin true repentance. Here a person must listen to a judgment such as this: "You are all of no account—whether you appear publicly to be sinners or saints. You must all become something different from what you are now and act in a different way, no matter who you are now and what you do. You may be as great, wise, powerful, and holy as you could want, but here no one is righteous, etc."

> To this office of the law, however, the New Testament immediately adds the consoling promises of grace, through the gospel. This we should believe. As Christ says in Mark 1(:15): "Repent, and believe in the good news." This is the same as, "Become and act otherwise, and believe my promise." Even before Jesus, John the Baptizer was called a preacher of repentance—but for the purpose of the forgiveness of sins. That is, John was to convict them all and turn them into sinners, so that they would know how they stood before God and would recognize themselves as lost people. In this way they were to be prepared for the Lord to receive grace, to await and accept from him forgiveness of sins. Jesus himself says in Luke 24(:47): "You must preach

repentance and forgiveness of sins in my name to the whole world."[4]

There is no good news in the Law, but it must be preached otherwise we would not know the depth of our depravity and our need for the forgiveness of sins that is bestowed in the Gospel alone. The Law must be proclaimed to those who live within the security of their sins. If the Gospel is preached to secure sinners, they will despise it or misuse it to confirm their own impenitence and unbelief. Sinners may be fixated on their self-made righteousness of good works or they may be living the lie that they are autonomous, free to do with their lives as they please. In either case, such sinners need the ministry of John the Baptist. Where the Law is not heard, there will be no repentance, only deepening security in legalism or lawlessness. To those who have been broken by their sins and crushed by the condemnation of the Law, the Gospel that alone pardons and comforts must have free course. The conscience bruised and bleeding needs no more Law, only Gospel. To such a person, we must speak as Luther did to his fellow friar, Spenlein:

> Therefore, my dear brother, learn Christ—Christ Crucified. Learn to sing praises to Him and to despair utterly of your own works. Say to Him: Thou, my Lord Jesus, art my Righteousness; I am Thy sin. Thou hast taken from me what is mine and hast given me what is Thine. Thou didst become what Thou wert not and madest me what I was not. Beware of your ceaseless striving after a righteousness so great that you no longer appear as a sinner in your own eyes and do not want to be a sinner. *For Christ dwells only in sinners.* He came down from heaven, where He dwelt in the righteous, for the very purpose of dwelling in sinners also. Ponder this love of His, and you will realize His sweetest consolation. (quoted in Walther, 110)

The distinction between Law and Gospel unravels when justification is made dependent on sanctification. We do not become holy people by doing holy things. It is the other way around. God justifies us, that is, He declares us to be holy and righteous for the sake of the suffering and death of His Son. God justifies the ungodly apart from works of the Law (see Romans 4:5). Salvation is a gift pure and simple, received by faith alone, not by human achievement. In his explanation of the twenty-fifth of his Heidelberg Theses of 1518, Luther says:

> For the righteousness of God is not acquired by means of acts frequently repeated, as Aristotle taught, but it is imparted by faith, for "He who through faith is righteous shall live" (Rom. 1:17), and "Man believes with his heart and so is justified" (Rom.10:10). Therefore I wish to have the words "without work" understood in the following manner: Not that the righteous person does nothing, but that his works do not make him righteous, rather that his righteousness creates works.[5]

Faith frees us from self-justification. Thinking and action are made new. Faith gives us a "new mind." Recognizing that we are righteous not on account of our works but on account of Christ's redeeming work, we now think differently about God, ourselves, and the world. There is no need to attempt to reach God on the basis of our moral strivings, the emotional intensity of our spiritual experiences, or the power of our rational thinking. In the forgiveness of sins we receive life and salvation as a gift through faith in Christ's promise. Freed from the curse of the Law, we are liberated for a life of good works. The world becomes the arena for vocation—our calling to live by faith under the cross and in loving service to the neighbor in his or her need. Writing in 1546 near the end of his life, Luther states in his "Preface to Romans": "Righteousness, then, is such a faith. It is called 'the righteousness of God' because God gives it, and counts it as righteousness for the sake of Christ our Mediator, and makes a man to fulfil his obligation to everybody. For through faith a man becomes free from sin and comes to take pleasure in God's commandments, thereby he gives God the honor due him, and pays what he owes him. Likewise he serves his fellow-men willingly, by whatever means he can and thus pays his debt to everyone."[6]

Christ has answered the curse of the Law by becoming a curse for us (see Galatians 3:13; 2 Corinthians 5:21). By His blood, He establishes peace between heaven and earth. Christ's sacrificial death for us has given us both deliverance from guilt and the strength for the new obedience. Justification is the basis and foundation for the life of sanctification. Oswald Bayer aptly demonstrates this by telling of the famous Lutheran hymn writer Paul Gerhardt:

> In his last will and testament Paul Gerhardt reminds his only son, still living after all his other children had died: "Do good to people, even if they cannot pay you back because . . . ." The reader expects that the sentence will continue with: "God *will* repay you." However, Paul Gerhardt frustrates that expectation by continuing: ". . . because for what human beings cannot repay, the Creator of heaven and earth *has* already repaid long ago when he created you, when he gave you his only Son, and when he accepted and received you in holy baptism as his child and heir."[7]

Freed from the curse of the Law through faith in Christ, the Christian is freed for the life of good works that God has prepared beforehand that we should walk in them (see Ephesians 2:8–10). Freedom from the Law does not produce antinomianism or lawlessness. It liberates the Christian to live within the concrete realities that are given us as creatures. As Reinhard Huetter puts it, "Christian freedom rejoices in God's commandments and welcomes them as creaturely ways of embodying our love of God and neighbor."[8]

Sanctification is always a return to justification. It is an error to make justification nothing more than an entryway to the renewed life as though forgiveness of sins was only needed initially and then one could move on to something greater, like sanctification. Paul puts an end to this false theology in Galatians 2:19–21: "For through the law I died to the law, so that I might live to God. I have been crucified with Christ. It is no longer I who live, but Christ who lives in me. And the life I now live in the flesh I live by faith in the Son of God, who loved me and gave himself for me. I do not nullify the grace of God, for if justification were through the law, then Christ died for no purpose." The apostle's words remind us of the truth of Adolph Köberle's warning that "it is not fitting to teach justification evangelically and then in the doctrine of sanctification to turn synergistic."[9] Both justification and sanctification are by faith.

The Christian life is best described in terms of circularity. We are always returning to the Gospel of the God who justifies the ungodly. In this life we do not outgrow our need for the forgiveness of sins. Einar Billing describes the Christian life as a continual movement between two poles, the forgiveness of sins and the Christian's daily calling in the world: "The whole process of sanctification goes on between those two poles, the forgiveness of sins, which continually restores us to our calling, and our calling, which continually refers us to the forgiveness of sins."[10] It is only through the gift of the forgiveness of sins—justification by grace through faith— that we remain connected to Jesus Christ. He says, "I am the vine; you are the branches. Whoever abides in Me and I in him, he it is that bears much fruit, for apart from Me you can do nothing" (John 15:5).

FOR REFLECTION AND DISCUSSION

1. List some contemporary examples of antinomianism. What does this false teaching do to the Gospel?

2. How is the proper distinction between the Law and the Gospel exhibited in Mark 1:15 and Acts 20:21?

3. Oswald Bayer says: "Faith is neither a theory nor praxis of self-fulfillment. It is a passive righteousness, namely, the work of God in us that we experience with suffering, dying both to justifying thinking and justifying action. By it rather, both thinking and action are renewed" (Oswald Bayer, *Living by Faith: Justification and Sanctification*, trans. G. W. Bromiley [Grand Rapids: Eerdmans, 2003], 25). How are Law and Gospel confused when faith is made a theory or praxis "of self-fulfillment"? See Ephesians 2:8–10.

4. Why is it necessary to distinguish justification from sanctification without separating the two? See John 15:1–8 and Galatians 2:19–21.

5. React to this statement: "Without the continual return to justification, sanctification falls into Pharisaism and the wildest exaggeration" (Adolph Köberle, *The Quest for Holiness*, trans. John C. Mattes [Minneapolis: Augsburg, 1938], 250).

6. How is sanctification a gift rather than a work of the Law? See 1 Corinthians 1:26–31, especially v. 30.

7. What happens when the Law is viewed as the source of the Christian life? See 2 Corinthians 3:4–6.

NOTES

1. Gerhard Forde, *On Being a Theologian of the Cross* (Grand Rapids: Eerdmans, 1997), x.

2. LW 47:111–13.

3. Gerhard Forde, "Fake Theology," *Dialog* (Fall 1983): 248.

4. Schmalkald Articles III, 3, 3–6 (K-W, 312–13).

5. LW 31:55–56.

6. LW 35:371.

7. Oswald Bayer, "Justification as Basis and Boundary for Theology," *Lutheran Quarterly* 15 (Autumn 2001): 276.

8. Reinhard Huetter, "Christian Freedom and God's Commandments," in *The Promise of Lutheran Ethics*, ed. K. Bloomquist and J. R. Stumme (Minneapolis: Fortress, 1998), 43.

9. Adolph Köberle, *The Quest for Holiness*, trans. John Mattes (Minneapolis: Augsburg, 1936), 95.

10. Einar Billing, *Our Calling*, trans. Conrad Bergendoff (Philadelphia: Fortress, 1964), 38.

Chapter Six

LOOKING IN ALL THE WRONG PLACES

In the fifth place, the Word of God is not rightly divided when sinners who have been struck down and terrified by the Law are directed, not to the Word and Sacraments, but to their own prayers and wrestlings with God in order that they may win their way into a state of grace; in other words, when they are told to keep on praying and struggling until they feel that God has received them into grace.—C. F. W. Walther (Thesis IX [Walther, 127])

Where is a person to look when he is terrified by a bad conscience that brings to remembrance the bitter knowledge of sin? Where is a person to look when she is searching for assurance of God's love and mercy? Where is a person to look when he is struck down by the Law and disarmed of every claim to righteousness? Where is the grace and mercy of God to be found? These are the questions that Walther addressed well over a century ago. They are still with us today.

Spirituality has become one of the code words of our generation. Seminars and self-help books offering a more profound sense of spirituality are in vogue these days. But spirituality is not to be confused with faith. We are not saved by our spirituality but through faith in Jesus Christ alone. Faith does not bubble up internally but is created by the Word that comes from outside of ourselves (see Romans 10:17). Jesus says: "If anyone loves Me, he will keep My word, and My Father will love him, and We will come and make Our home with him. Whoever does not love Me does not keep My words. And the word that you hear is not Mine but the Father's who sent Me" (John 14:23–24). Here we see the real difference between human spirituality and faith.

Spirituality is anchored in the human heart—that heart the prophet Jeremiah describes as "deceitful above all things" (Jeremiah 17:9). It is a heart that cannot be trusted, for it is a fountain that spews forth evil thoughts, murder, adultery, and lies, says Jesus (see Matthew 15:19). The human heart prefers its own enthusiasms rather than God's Word. Like Eve in Eden's garden, the heart gravitates toward what it can see and experience. Departing from the words God had spoken, Eve embraced the words of the serpent. These deceitful and deceiving words promised that she would be "like God" (Genesis 3:5). The serpent lied. Luther saw this satanic strategy in those preachers of his day who wanted to be more spiritual than the Holy Spirit: "In these matters, which concern the spoken, external Word, it must be firmly maintained that God gives no one his Spirit or grace apart from the external Word which goes before. We say this to protect ourselves from the enthusiasts, that is, the 'spirits,' who boast that they have the Spirit apart from and before contact with the Word. On this basis, they judge, interpret, and twist the Scriptures or oral Word according to their pleasure."[1]

Unlike the preaching of the ancient serpent, preachers sent by God direct their hearers away from the imaginations of the human heart and to the truth of the Lord's means of grace: the preached Word, Baptism, Absolution, and the Lord's Supper. Walther illustrates this point by turning to Acts 2, the narrative of Pentecost. The apostle Peter rehearses the story of Jesus' life, passion, resurrection, and ascension. Then comes the clincher: "Let all the house of Israel therefore know for certain that God has made Him both Lord and Christ, this Jesus whom you crucified" (Acts 2:36). Luke reports that the Jews who heard this sermon "were cut to the heart" and inquired "what shall we do?" (Acts 2:37). Peter did not counsel his hearers to turn inward to their own prayers and spiritual struggling. Nor did he call them to amend their sinful lives so God might have pity on them. Rather, Peter said: "Repent and be baptized every one of you in the name of Jesus Christ for the forgiveness of your sins, and you will receive the gift of the Holy Spirit" (Acts 2:38). Peter simply called his hearers to repentance and Baptism. Walther says, "That is the whole story. Other demands the apostle did not make; his hearers were only to listen to his words and take comfort in these soothing words of consolation, this promise of the forgiveness of their sins, of life and salvation. We are not told about measures such as the sects in our day employ" (Walther, 129).

No doubt that Walther had in mind the evangelists such as Charles Finney (1792–1875), who were associated with the Second Great Awakening. Finney's *Systematic Theology* argued that conversion was not an act of God but a human response prompted by nothing more than "the right use of means."[2] Some Lutherans, such as Samuel Simon Schmucker (1799–1873) and Benjamin Kurtz (1795–1865), adopted these revivalistic techniques, known as the "new measures," in their efforts to make the Lutheran church evangelistically effective in North America.

The revivalists of Walther's day worked their audiences into a spiritual frenzy, probing the depths of the soul to uncover any hidden sin and directing those who were "awakened" to intensified struggle and fervent prayer. Only through such agony could one arrive at the assurance of a genuine conversion, it was thought. The old revivalists have a modern counterpart in the television evangelists and megachurch preachers who are skilled at using techniques to work their hearers through spiritual laws or programs culminating in a heartfelt decision to offer one's heart to Jesus in prayer. Law and Gospel are confused, for feelings are equated with faith, human emotion with God's truth. Craig Parton spent seven years as a full-time staff member of Campus Crusade for Christ, yet he points out that Evangelicalism left him without the comforting news that Jesus' atonement remains as the foundation and source of the Christian life. Instead, he was left under the demand of the Law. He says:

> I experienced what happens when Law and Gospel are not understood and thus not distinguished. My Christian life, truly begun in grace, was now being "perfected" on the treadmill of the Law. My pastors did not end their sermons by demanding that I recite the rosary or visit Lourdes that week in order to unleash God's power; instead, I was told to yield more, pray more, care more about unbelievers, read the Bible more, get involved with the church more, and love my wife and kids more. Not until I came to the Lutheran Reformation some 20 years later, did I understand that my Christian life had come to center around my life, my obedience, my yielding, my Bible verse memorization, my prayers, my zeal, my witnessing, and my sermon application. I had advanced beyond the need to hear the cross preached to me anymore . . . . What had my Evangelical training done to me? The Gospel was critical for me at the beginning, critical to now share with others, and still critical to get me to heaven, but it was of little other value. The "evangel" in Evangelicalism was missing. My Evangelical training had me on a treadmill of merit. My "solid Bible training" was killing me.[3]

The cross and the forgiveness of sins are assumed, but the real focus is on Christian experience and works. Parton's experience of modern Evangelicalism is not that distant from the Revivalism that confronted Walther more than a century and a half ago.

Walther observes that the preaching of American Evangelicalism is based on three errors. First, there is a denial of the complete reconciliation of humanity with God through the saving death of Jesus Christ. Walther says that this "amounts to a denial of Jesus Christ, who long ago turned the heart of God to men by reconciling the entire world with Him" (Walther, 135). Redemption is complete. The sins of the world are blotted out in the blood of Christ (see Romans 3:23–26; 2 Corinthians 5:14–21). The atonement of Jesus Christ is universal; it covers Adam and all of his descendents. Walther says: "If Christ died for the sins of all men, that is tantamount to all men's dying and making satisfaction for their sins. Therefore nothing at all is required on the part of man to reconcile God; He is already reconciled. Righteousness lies ready; it must not first be achieved by man" (Walther, 136). The finished work of Jesus Christ is the only foundation for speaking the Gospel. Walther says, "God does nothing by halves" (Walther, 136). Our Lord's triumphant cry, "It is finished" (John 19:30), gives us the certainty of salvation accomplished outside of our doing. There are no missing pieces of the puzzle for us to add.

Second, Walther observes that "the sects teach false doctrine concerning the Gospel" (Walther, 136). Here Walther refers to those who see the Gospel as spiritual principles that, if implemented, will lead to life with God. Rather than announcing and declaring the forgiveness of sins for Christ's sake, this type of preaching turns the Gospel into a conditional promise. It is conditioned on some work or disposition in the heart of the hearer. Not so Lutheran preaching! Genuine Lutheran preachers are bound to speak a word of promise without the ifs, ands, and buts that turn the good news of Jesus into another Law. In the grammar of the Gospel, God carries the action of the verbs. He calls into being that which does not exist. His Word declares the unrighteous righteous and causes the dead to live!

Third, Walther states that "the sects teach false doctrine concerning faith" (Walther, 136). He faults the sectarian preachers of making faith into a work, something that we must do to be saved. Faith is made into a rational decision. But this is not the biblical understanding of faith. Walther explains the story of the conversion of the prison guard in Acts 16:25–34 like this: "The Scriptural answer to the question: 'What must I do to be saved?' is: 'You must believe; hence you are not to do anything at all yourself.' . . . He practically told the jailer: 'You are to do nothing but accept what God has done for you, and you have it and become a blessed person'" (Walther, 137). Faith contributes nothing to salvation. Faith is passive, receiving only what Christ gives. Robin Leaver says,

> Luther's doctrine of justification by faith alone can only be truly appreciated if his theology of creation is understood. For him creation is *ex nihilo*—out of nothing . . . "When God creates faith in a man, this is as great a work as if He were to create heaven and earth again." [LW 30:14] As in God's original creation the creature could not and did not assist the Creator in His bringing it into existence, so in God's re-creation by His Spirit, man is remolded and refashioned without his cooperation: It is entirely the work of God through His Spirit.[4]

Faith clings to Jesus Christ. Where is Jesus? He is where He has promised to be for us—in His Word, in Baptism, in the Holy Supper, and in Absolution. Jesus' words are not dead letters; they are "spirit and life" (John 6:63). His words say what they do and they do what they say. God's Spirit and Word go together. "By the word of the LORD the heavens were made, and by the breath of His mouth all their host," says the psalmist (Psalm 33:6). The Lord who spoke creation into existence is speaking still, and the words that He breathes out do not return to Him empty. They accomplish His purpose (see Isaiah 55:11).

God's Word joined to the water washes away sin in Holy Baptism. Walther says: "According to the Holy Scriptures, Baptism is not a mere washing with earthly water, but the Spirit of God, yea, Jesus with His blood, connects with it for the purpose of cleansing me of my sins" (Walther, 151). Baptism saves because it joins sinners to Jesus' death (see Romans 6:1–11; 1 Peter 3:21). As Luther says: "Baptism, then, signifies two things—death and resurrection, that is, full and complete justification. . . . This death and resurrection we call the new creation, regeneration, and spiritual birth. This should not be understood only allegorically as the death of sin and the life of grace, as many understand it, but as actual death and res-urrection. For baptism is not a false sign."[5]

Baptism is God's work, as we see from the biblical language of rebirth or regeneration (see Titus 3:5–8). No one gives birth to him-self or wills his own birth. Birth is something that is given (see John 3:5–6). Here we may adduce a comment from Luther to the effect that Baptism is not to be seen as a human ceremony: "Thus you see plainly that baptism is not a work that we do but that it is a treasure that God gives us and faith grasps, just as the LORD Christ upon the cross is not a work but a treasure placed in the setting of the Word and offered us in the Word and received by faith."[6] Baptism as God's work can be most clearly seen from the gifts He bestows in Baptism: forgiveness of sins and the Holy Spirit (Acts 2:38–39).

The Lord's Supper is no earthly meal but the banquet of the new testament, the body and blood of Jesus given and shed for the forgiveness of sins. We call this Sacrament the Lord's Supper because the Lord Himself is host at this Holy Feast. In this Supper, the Lord gives us His body to eat and His blood to drink. The Lord's Supper is not a sacrifice that we offer to God but the Sacrament in which He feeds us with the fruits of Jesus' sacrifice on the cross, His body and blood. Believing sinners find comfort in the Sacrament, for here Christ Himself delivers the forgiveness won on Good Fri-day. Luther put it like this: "If now I seek the forgiveness of sins, I do not run to the cross, for I will not find it there. Nor must I hold to the suffering of Christ, as Dr. Karlstadt trifles, in knowledge or remembrance, for I will not find it there either. But I will find in the sacrament or gospel the word which distributes, presents, offers and gives to me that forgiveness which was won on the cross."[7]

The absolution that Christ speaks in sermon and Sacrament is no pious wish but the reality of sins actually forgiven. The words on the lips of Christ's servants "I forgive you all your sins in the name of the Father and of the Son and of the Holy Spirit" is the forgive-ness of God Himself. This is the forgiveness that the Lord commis-sioned His apostles to deliver on Easter evening (see John

20:19–23). The forgiveness won on Calvary where God was in Christ making peace through the blood of the cross is now given to the apostles to deliver. Forgiveness of sins is located in Jesus' words that unlock the chains that bind us and frees us for life with God forever.

The Gospel done at Calvary in the death of Jesus is now delivered in the means of grace. Thus Luther writes in the Large Catechism:

> Neither you nor I could ever know anything about Christ, or believe in him and receive him as Lord, unless these were offered to us and bestowed on our hearts through the preaching of the gospel by the Holy Spirit. The work is finished and completed; Christ has acquired and won the treasure for us by his sufferings, death, and resurrection, etc. But if the work remained hidden so that no one knew of it, it would have been all in vain, all lost. In order that this treasure might not remain buried but be put to use and enjoyed, God has caused the Word to be published and proclaimed, in which he has given the Holy Spirit to offer and apply to us this treasure, this redemption.[8]

Our God is no distant deity. He is not watching us from a distance to see if we can find our way to life with Him. Rather, He comes to us to set our hearts at peace with His forgiveness. His mighty Word that calmed the chaos of wind and wave now comforts us with the knowledge that our sins are erased by Jesus' blood. Our future is that of the empty tomb.

Faith is grounded on God's Word, not on fickle feelings and elusive emotions. God gives us His Word and Sacraments—gifts that are outside of ourselves—that we might have confidence in life and in death. This is a confidence that will not disappoint because it is of Christ.

FOR REFLECTION AND DISCUSSION

1. What is the difference between spirituality and faith?

2. The language of the heart has become prominent in our day. Why

is the heart unreliable? See Jeremiah 17:9 and Matthew 15:19.

3. Read Acts 2:22–41. How does Peter proclaim Law in this sermon? How does he preach the Gospel? Where does he direct his hearers after they had been "cut to the heart" with his preaching?

4. How is the completed atonement of Christ the basis for the preaching of absolution? See 2 Corinthians 5:14–21 and Romans 3:23–26.

5. How does Christ deliver the gifts of His redemption? See John 20:19–23; Titus 3:5–8; and 1 Corinthians 11:23–26.

6. How does Lutheran preaching differ from the preaching of American Evangelicalism? Why must the proclamation of the forgiveness of sins always predominate in the Christian sermon? What happens when some other goal for the sermon takes priority?

NOTES

1. Schmalkald Articles III, 8 (K-W, 322).

2. Quoted in Michael S. Horton, *Made in America: The Shaping of Modern American Evangelicalism* (Grand Rapids: Baker, 1991), 44–45.

3. Craig A. Parton, *The Defense Never Rests: A Lawyer's Quest for the Gospel* (St. Louis: Concordia, 2003), 18.

4. Robin Leaver, *Luther on Justification* (St. Louis: Concordia, 1975), 32.

5. LW 36:67–68.

6. Large Catechism IV, "Baptism," 37 (K-W, 461).

7. LW 40:214.

8. Large Catechism, "The Creed," 38 (K-W, 436).

Chapter Seven

BY FAITH ALONE

In the sixth place, the Word of God is not rightly divided when the preacher describes faith in a manner as if the mere inert acceptance of truths, even while a person is living in mortal sins, renders that person righteous in the sight of God and saves him; or as if faith makes a person righteous and saves him for the reason that it produces in him love and reformation of his mode of living.—C. F. W. Walther (Thesis X [Walther, 210])

In the eighth place, the Word of God is not rightly divided when the preacher represents contrition alongside of faith as a cause of the forgiveness of sin.—C. F. W. Walther (Thesis XII [Walther, 249])

In the ninth place, the Word of God is not rightly divided when one makes an appeal to believe in a manner as if a person could make himself believe or at least help toward that end, instead of preaching faith into a person's heart by laying the Gospel promises before him.—C. F. W. Walther (Thesis XIII [Walther, 260])

In the tenth place, the Word of God is not rightly divided when faith is required as a condition of justification and salvation, as if a person were righteous in the sight of God and saved, not only by faith, but also on account of his

faith, for the sake of his faith, and in view of his faith.—
C. F. W. Walther (Thesis XIV [Walther, 268])

What is faith? Is faith just believing that certain facts are true, as a person might be confident that George Washington was the first president of the United States? Is faith a self-generated conviction of optimism? Is it a personal conviction that produces commitment to a particular cause? Faith defined as something accomplished by man undermines the work of Christ, throwing us back on our own energy or efforts. Against all definitions that see faith as something done by man, Walther asserts: "What God's Word really means when it says that man is justified and saved by faith alone is nothing else than this: Man is *not saved by his own acts,* but *solely* by the doing and dying of his Lord and Savior Jesus Christ, the Redeemer of the whole world" (Walther, 269, *Walther's emphasis*).

In a way reminiscent of Luther's "Theses Concerning Faith and Law" written in 1535, Walther argues that saving faith is not to be confused with merely believing certain truths. Luther addressed this problem: "If Paul is understood to be speaking of acquired or historic faith (in Romans 3:28), he is laboring entirely in vain. . . . if you understand Paul to be speaking of this kind of faith, he is preaching about an idle and fictitious Christ . . . he is necessarily speaking of another kind of faith which shall make Christ effective in us against death, sin, and the law."[1] This "historical faith" is no better than the knowledge possessed by the devils. As James says, "You believe that God is one; you do well. Even the demons believe—and shudder!" (James 2:19). Saving faith, on the other hand, believes God's word of truth as the true and efficacious promises that He extends to sinners. This is exactly the point made in the Augsburg Confession: "People are also reminded that the term 'faith' here does not signify only historical knowledge—the kind of faith that the ungodly and the devil have—but that it signifies faith which believes not only the history but also the effect of history, namely, this article of the forgiveness of sins, that is, that we have grace, righteousness, and forgiveness of sins through Christ."[2] Faith is trust that all of God's promises in Christ are for me.

This faith is not formed by love. Faith is not completed or supplemented by works. When it comes to salvation, faith remains utterly alone. What then of love and the works of love? Walther answers:

> The inefficiency of a faith that fails to work by love is not due to a lack of love, but to the fact that it is not real, honest faith. Love must not be added to faith but grow out of it. A fruitful tree does not produce fruit by somebody's order, but because, while there is vitality in it and it is not dried up, it must produce fruit spontaneously. Faith is such a tree; it proves its vitality by bearing fruit. It is withered when it fails to bring forth fruit. The sun, likewise, need not be told to shine, it will continue shining till Judgment Day without any one's issuing orders to do it. Faith is such a sun. (Walther, 211)

Faith does not save by making us do works that are worthy of salvation. Faith saves by apprehending the Savior. He alone is the source of all good works in the life of the Christian. Walther says: "Far from placing good works in the background, the doctrine of the Lutheran Church points to the true source from which good works must spring. For a person who by the Holy Spirit and the grace of God has obtained a living confidence in Christ cannot abide in sin. His faith changes and purifies his heart" (Walther, 213–14). This can be seen from 1 Corinthians 6:9–11 where Paul says: "Do you not know that the unrighteous will not inherit the kingdom of God? Do not be deceived; neither the sexually immoral, nor idolaters, nor adulterers, nor men who practice homosexuality, nor thieves, nor the greedy, nor drunkards, nor revilers, nor swindlers will inherit the kingdom of God. And such were some of you. But you were washed, you were sanctified, you were justified in the name of the Lord Jesus Christ and by the Spirit of our God." The apostle Paul anticipates and intercepts the suggestion that God's abundant grace in the justification of the ungodly is permission for the old life. He quickly denounces such a move in Romans 6:1–2: "What shall we say then? Are we to continue in sin that grace may abound? By no means! How can we who died to sin still live in it?"

Justification by faith is not the justification of sin. Dying to sin, the believer is made alive for a life of love that flows from faith in Jesus Christ. Luther says:

> All who boast of works to justify themselves in the eyes of God show that they understand nothing about Christ or faith. We confess that good works must follow faith, yes, not only must, but follow voluntarily, just as a good tree not only must produce good fruits, but does so freely (Matt. 7:18). Just as good fruits do not make the tree good, so good works do not justify the person. But good works come from a person who has already been justified beforehand by faith, just as good fruits come from a tree which is already good beforehand by nature.[3]

We are not saved on account of our contrition, our sorrow over sin. Contrition or repentance as described by Walther is not a spiritual condition created by human beings. True, without repentance there is no faith. This is why Jesus charges His apostles to preach repentance and the forgiveness of sins (Luke 24:46–47). Repentance is the recognition of one's need for a Savior. Those who fancy themselves as healthy do not see themselves in need of a physician (Matthew 9:12–13). "As long as a person has not been reduced to the state of a poor, lost, and condemned sinner, he has no serious interest in the Savior of sinners" (Walther, 249).

Repentance is not a cause of forgiveness, but it is only in repentance that a person will apprehend Christ by faith. When repentance is made a cause of faith, Law and Gospel are mingled in two ways according to Walther. First, to regard repentance as a cause of forgiveness of sins turns "the Law into a message of grace and the Gospel into Law—a perversion which overthrows the entire Christian religion" (Walther, 250). Second, repentance is not a good work performed by us.

For the contrition which precedes faith is nothing but suffering on the part of man. It consists of anguish, pain, torment, a feeling of being crushed; all of which God has wrought in man with the hammer of the Law. It is not an anguish which a person has produced in himself, for he would gladly be rid of it, but cannot, because God has come down on him with the Law, and he sees no way of escape from the ordeal. If a person sits down to meditate with a view to producing contrition in himself, he will never gain his object that way. He cannot produce contrition. Those who think that they can are miserable hypocrites. They seek to persuade themselves that they have contrition, but it is not so. Genuine repentance is produced by God only when the Law is preached in all sternness and man does not willfully resist its influence. (Walther, 250)

Contrition cannot be measured in terms of quality or quantity. Walther says, "If one has the desire to come to Jesus, he has true contrition even if he does not feel it" (Walther, 251). There is no checklist of experiences that one may use to ascertain the genuineness of repentance. The troubled sinner is not directed to inward lamentation or outward amendment of life. There are no penitential exercises to perform. To repent is to be crushed by the Law, as David was when he confessed to Nathan, "I have sinned against the LORD" (2 Samuel 12:13). Exposed in his sin, David had no place to turn but to the mercy of God. This is the forgiveness proclaimed in the absolution uttered by Nathan: "The LORD also has put away your sin; you shall not die" (2 Samuel 12:13).

It is the Gospel, not the Law, that brings forgiveness of sins. Walther warns against preaching faith in such a way that makes the Gospel a demand rather than an invitation. "When demanding faith, we do not lay down a demand of the Law, but issue the sweetest invitation, practically saying to our hearers: 'Come, for all things are now ready.' Luke 14,17. When I invite a half-starved person to sit down to a well-furnished board and to help himself to anything he likes, I do not expect him to tell me that he will take no orders from me. Even so the demand to believe is to be understood not as an order of the Law, but an invitation of the Gospel" (Walther, 260).

Bo Giertz, in the novel we have discussed, tells the story of a young pastor who thought of faith as obedience to the Law's demand. He wanted to make sure that his senior pastor recognized that "he had given his heart to Jesus" and was, therefore, a "real believer." The old pastor responds to the young cleric's proud confidence:

> "[I]f you think you are saved because you give Jesus your heart, you will not be saved. You see, my boy," he continued reassuringly, as he continued to look at the young pastor's face, in which uncertainty and resentment were shown in the struggle for the upper hand, "it is *one thing* to choose Jesus as one's Lord and Savior, to give Him your heart and commit oneself to Him, and that He now accepts one into His little flock; it is a very different thing to believe in Him as Redeemer of sinners, of whom one is chief. One does not choose a Redeemer for oneself, you understand, nor give one's heart to Him. The heart is a rusty old can on a junk heap. A fine birthday gift, indeed! But a wonderful Lord passes by, and has mercy on that wretched tin can, sticks his walking cane through it and rescues it from the junk pile and takes it home with Him. That is how it is."[4] (*Giertz's emphasis*)

Faith is not a commitment that we can muster. Faith is not doing our part. Faith is not a decision that we make for Christ. Faith is that trust in the mercy of God in Jesus Christ that is created by the promises of God. Lutheran pastors preach faith by preaching the Gospel. This is what Walther means when he says faith is preached "into a person's heart by laying the Gospel promises before him" (Walther, 260). Jesus' words illustrate this as He says to His disciples, "You did not choose Me, but I chose you and appointed you that you should go and bear fruit and that your fruit should abide, so that whatever you ask the Father in My name, He may give it to you" (John 15:16). Faith is not a choice that we make. Faith is God's gift that makes alive those who are dead in sin. Corpses cannot choose to be made alive.

When faith is described as our commitment, duty, or decision, we are thrown back to our own resources. That leaves us in uncertainty. Walther recognized those in his day who would speak of salvation by faith alone yet missed the mark: "But by faith they understand nothing but what man himself achieves and produces. Their faith is a product of human energy and resolution. Such teaching, however, subverts the entire Gospel" (Walther, 268–69). Faith is not a condition of salvation but simply trust in God's *promises*—trust that receives the gift. "Faith," says Luther, "is a living, daring confidence in God's grace, so sure and certain that the believer would stake his life on it a thousand times. It is more sure and certain than all experience and life itself."[5] The Gospel is received by faith alone, "that the promise may rest on grace" (Romans 4:16). In other words, "faith is not an achievement of ours, but is wrought in us by God without our contributing anything towards that end" (Walther, 273).

FOR REFLECTION AND DISCUSSION

1. What is the difference between "historic faith" and "saving faith"? See James 2:19.

2. Read the story of Zacchaeus in Luke 19:1–10. How are Law and Gospel at work in this episode?

3. Read Ephesians 2:1–10. How is faith defined in this text in such a way as to exclude the definition of faith as a human work? Recall Luther's Explanation to the Third Article of the Creed in the Small Catechism.

4. Read Romans 4:1–17. Abraham was justified by faith, not by works. How does Paul argue this point? What is the significance of Paul's argument for the proper distinction of Law and Gospel?

5. One irreverent person has said: "The world is wonderfully arranged. God loves to forgive and I love to sin." Using 1 Corinthians 6:9–11 and Romans 6:1–2, how would you answer this claim?

6. What happens when faith is confused with commitment?

NOTES

1. Quoted in Robin Leaver, *Luther on Justification* (St. Louis: Concordia, 1975), 29.

2. Augsburg Confession XX, 23 (K-W, 57).

3. LW 34:111.

4. Bo Giertz, *The Hammer of God*, trans. Clifford A. Nelson (Minneapolis: Augsburg, 1973), 147.

5. Oswald Bayer, "Justification as Basis and Boundary for Theology," *Lutheran Quarterly* 15 (Autumn 2001): 26.

Chapter Eight

RIGHT REPENTANCE

In the seventh place, the Word of God is not rightly divided when there is a disposition to offer the comfort of the Gospel only to those who have been made contrite by the Law, not from fear of the wrath and punishment of God, but from the love of God.—C. F. W. Walther (Thesis XI [Walther, 236])

In the eleventh place, the Word of God is not rightly divided when the Gospel is turned into the preaching of repentance.—C. F. W. Walther (Thesis XV [Walther, 277])

In the twelfth place, the Word of God is not rightly divided when the preacher tries to make people believe that they are truly converted as soon as they have become rid of certain vices and engage in certain works of piety and virtuous practises.—C. F. W. Walther (Thesis XVI [Walther, 299])

In the thirteenth place, the Word of God is not rightly divided when a description is given of faith, both as regards to its strength and the consciousness and productiveness of it, that does not fit all believers at all times.—C. F. W. Walther (Thesis XVII [Walther, 308])

The Law is a powerful word. It has the power to crush and to kill, to convict and to condemn. But the Law is absolutely impotent to give life and renew. The Law can uncover our lack of love for God, but it is powerless to create this love. Walther says:

> Since the Fall the Law, you know, has but a single function . . . to lead men to the knowledge of their sins. It has no power to renew them. That power is vested solely in the Gospel. Only faith worketh by love; we do not become spiritually active by love, by sorrow over our sins. On the contrary, while still ignorant of the fact that God has become our reconciled God and Father through Christ, we hate Him. An unconverted person who claims that he loves God is stating an untruth and is guilty of a miserable piece of hypocrisy, though he may not be conscious of it. He sets up a specious claim, because only faith in the Gospel regenerates a person. Accordingly, a person cannot love God while he is still without faith. To demand of a poor sinner that he must, from the love of God, be alarmed on account of his sins and feel sorry for them is an abominable perversion of Law and Gospel. (Walther, 236)

Far from working the love of God in the heart, the Law actually does the opposite. It works the wrath of God (Romans 4:15), arouses sin itself (Romans 7:7–8), and causes sin to abound (Romans 5:20). The Law can and does kill, but only the Spirit at work in the Gospel gives life (see 2 Corinthians 3:6). Peter's hearers at Pentecost were cut to the heart with fear and terror, not because of the preaching of God's love but because the preaching of the Law identified them as those who had committed messianic murder (see Acts 2:22–41).

This was Luther's experience in the monastery. The more he struggled to meet the demand of the Law that he love God above all things, the more he found himself terrorized by his hatred of God. Haunted by the realization that he could not attain to "the righteousness of God," Luther could only conclude that he was not one of the elect. God Himself was the source of Luther's sorrow. It was only as Luther came to see from the Scriptures that God's righteousness is not something that one achieves but that it is received through faith in Christ alone that his heart was set at peace.

Real repentance, that is, the terror of conscience on account of sin, is not something that a person can produce in the self. It is produced only as the Law does its work, hammering away at everything that a sinner seeks to cling to for security and comfort that is not of Jesus Christ. Here Walther draws on 2 Corinthians 7:10 as the apostle Paul makes a distinction between "godly grief" and "worldly grief." Godly grief is the sorrow that God produces.

> There is not in all the world a person who can produce contrition in himself. He may labor to bring it forth until he becomes dissolved in tears, but it is all a hypocritical sham. *Godly* sorrow is required because faith is required. God, by terrifying us, wants to produce this sorrow. We must not imagine that contrition is a good work which we do, but something that God works in us. God comes with the hammer of the Law and smites our soul. A person who wants to make himself sorrowful desires ever to increase his sorrow over sin. But a person merged in the right kind of sorrow yearns to be rid of it. (Walther, 240, *Walther's emphasis*)

Worldly grief frets over earthly loss and mourns over temporal suffering that might result from a broken body, a damaged reputation, or a civil penalty. Godly grief laments hell itself. Walther wisely cautions against attempting to ferret out motivation when it comes to repentance. "It is impossible to ascertain the motive of a person's contrition. No matter what it is: when we behold some one in terror of hell, we are to comfort him" (Walther, 241). Such a person does not need intrusive probing from the Law but the consolation of the Gospel.

> When you preach, do not be stingy with the Gospel; bring its consolations to all, even to the greatest sinners. When they are terrified by the wrath of God and hell, they are fully prepared to receive the Gospel. True, this goes against our reason; we think it strange that such knaves are to be comforted immediately; we imagine they ought to be made to suffer much greater agony in their conscience. Fanatics adopt that method in dealing with alarmed sinners; but a

genuine Bible theologian resolves to preach the Gospel and faith in Jesus Christ to a person whom God has prepared for such preaching by His Law. (Walther, 240)

The Gospel is not the preaching of repentance but the proclamation of the forgiveness of sins. Here Walther draws on traditional dogmatic distinctions between the "wide" and the "narrow" senses of both the Gospel and repentance. In the broad sense, the word *Gospel* can mean the entirety of God's Word, while in the narrow sense, it means the words of God that promise forgiveness of sins. Likewise, *repentance* in the broad sense indicates both the turning from sin and the embrace of Christ by faith, while in the narrow sense, it refers only to sorrow or contrition on account of sin. The preaching of repentance in the narrow sense is the preaching of the Law. The preaching of the Gospel in the narrow sense is nothing but the proclamation of the forgiveness of sins on account of Jesus Christ.

Antinomians (see chapter 5) ancient and modern have dismissed the Law only to end up with a legalized Gospel. That is no good news at all. The Gospel is transformed from pure gift to strict demand. No longer is the Gospel "the power of God for salvation" (Romans 1:16), but it is made into a demand for discipleship, a new law. Antinomianism hides Christ behind the veil of Moses (see 2 Corinthians 3–4), and it drives sinners either to the damnable self-confidence of the Pharisees or to the despair of a wretched Judas. It is against this deadly misstep that the Formula of Concord seeks to guard Christian preaching:

> When, however, law and gospel are placed in contrast to each other—as when Moses himself is spoken of as a teacher of the law and Christ as a preacher of the gospel—we believe, teach, and confess that the gospel is not a proclamation of repentance or retribution, but is, strictly speaking, nothing else than a proclamation of comfort and a joyous message which does not rebuke nor terrify but comforts consciences against the terror of the law, directs them solely to Christ's merit, and lifts them up again

through the delightful proclamation of the grace and favor
of God, won through Christ's merit.[1]

The Law reproves sin but does not forgive it. The Gospel does not
reprove sin but forgives it on the authority of Christ's atonement.

Without this distinction, we will misread the Holy Scriptures.
Drawing on Luther's "Prefaces to the New Testament,"[2] Walther
demonstrates how the reformer uses the right distinction of Law
and Gospel to read the Bible correctly as it gets us to the very heart
of the Scriptures: Jesus Christ crucified and risen for sinners.

> You must proclaim the Law forcefully; your pulpit must
> reverberate with its thunder and lightning. But the moment
> you begin to speak of the Gospel, the Law must be hushed.
> Moses set up a barrier around Mount Sinai, but Christ and
> the apostles placed no barrier around Golgotha. Here
> everybody is accorded free access. The person approaching
> the God of the Law must be righteous; the person
> approaching the reconciling God on Golgotha may come
> just as he is. Yea, he is welcome for the very reason that he
> is a sinner, if he will but come. (Walther, 291)

The Law makes sinners, but the Gospel takes sinners and
declares them to be saints, holy and righteous through faith in Jesus
Christ. This is why the Gospel is pictured as the preaching of peace
to those who are estranged from God (see Ephesians 2:14–17) and
good news to the poor who have nothing to contribute to their salvation (Luke 4:18–19). It is not the work of human beings but of
God. This definition of the Gospel prompts Walther to write
against any commingling of Law and Gospel, for such a mixing
would turn the Gospel into Law.

This happens with every rationalistic belief system that con-
fuses repentance with behavior modification. Bad habits may be
overcome by strength of will and self-discipline. With persistent
effort, annoying vices may be replaced by wholesome virtues. Techniques may change outward behavior, but faith alone changes the
heart. The call to repentance is the call for a changed heart, the call
to become what you are not. When the Lord says, "Repent," Walther

explains, "the Lord confronts the sinner, telling him that, first of all, a change of the innermost self must take place. What He requires is a new mind, a new heart, a new spirit; not quitting vice and doing good works. By making this the primary requisite for being Christian, He puts the ax to the root of the evil tree" (Walther, 300). God is looking for the fruits of repentance, not decorative fruit artificially attached to a lifeless tree.

Jesus says that good fruit is produced by a good tree (see Matthew 12:33). Drawing on Jesus' words, Walther says: "Plant a good tree, and it will bear good fruit; plant a corrupt tree, and it will bear corrupt fruit. This means: Unless a person is completely changed, unless he has become a new creature, has been born anew, with a new mind, all his doings will be corrupt fruit; for by nature every man is a corrupt tree" (Walther, 301). This is what Paul means in Romans 14:23 when he says, "For whatever does not proceed from faith is sin." Virtues may be praiseworthy and beneficial when it comes to life in human community, but virtues do not save us from God's wrath. That is the job of Christ alone; the benefits of His redeeming work on the cross are received by faith alone.

Walther uses the story of Nicodemus in John 3 to illustrate the impossibility of the sinner doing anything that would bring salvation. When Nicodemus confesses Jesus as a "teacher come from God," Jesus answers him, "Truly, truly, I say to you, unless one is born again he cannot see the kingdom of God" (John 3:2–3). How can a man be born again? Such a thought is impossible. Gerhard Forde comments that Nicodemus is the theologian of glory *par excellence*. "The theologian of glory has at last come up against something that can't be done!"[3] Any change will not come from Nicodemus's strivings after spirituality or his embrace of virtue. Nicodemus must become a new man. Just as physical birth is not a matter of human choice, so the new birth is not by human effort. It is the work of God. "You must consider yourself an unborn infant, who is not only unable to do a single good work, but has not even attained to life and being as yet. That is what Christians preach. The

Christian doctrine teaches us that we must first become different people, that is, we must be born again. How is this done? By the Holy Spirit and by the water of Baptism. After I have been born again and have been made godly and God-fearing, I begin a new life, and what I do now, in my regenerate state, is good" (Walther, 304). The work is good because the doer is good, that is, a sinner is now covered by the righteousness of another, Jesus Christ the Righteous One. Good works come naturally for the person who is in Christ, just as a good tree will produce abundant fruit.

Born from above, the Christian is a new being. But that does not mean that Christians are without sin. The struggle against sin continues. Paul describes the battle that rages on in the Christian life: "For I know that nothing good dwells in me, that is, in my flesh. For I have the desire to do what is right, but not the ability to carry it out. For I do not do the good I want, but the evil I do not want is what I keep on doing" (Romans 7:18–19). Law and Gospel are confused when faith is described in such a way that it "does not fit all believers at all times" (Walther, 308). In other words, faith must not be defined in such a way that does not take into account the fact that the Christian is simultaneously both saint and sinner, "a double being" (Walther, 309) or *simul iustus et peccator*, as Luther put it.

The reference point is not on the strength or productivity of our faith *per se* but on the content of faith—the sure promises of God in Jesus Christ. The confidence of the Christian is not in his emotions, the intensity of the sensations of security and happiness. Spiritual euphoria is not a sign of faith. Faith is not determined by disposition. "Furthermore, you must bear in mind that a Christian retains his natural temperament even after his conversion. A person with an irritable temper keeps that disposition, and it may frequently get the better of him. You must not say, then, that when a person becomes a Christian, he turned from a bear into a lamb, in the sense that he is willing to take scolding and scorn from everybody and is always ready to forgive his fellow-men" (Walther, 312–13). Christians continue to face dark temptations and stumble into sin. The life of faith may never be described as a life without sin but a life that is lived trusting in the forgiveness of sins that Christ bestows. On the strength of that gift, the Christian is armed for an ongoing battle against the flesh.

FOR REFLECTION AND DISCUSSION

1. How does the Law manifest its power? See Romans 4:15; Romans 5:20; Romans 7:7–8; and 2 Corinthians 3:6.

2. In his dispute with John Agricola, Luther says: "For a man, terrified by the form of sin, cannot intend the good by his own powers, since he can neither be quieted nor secured. But confused and ruined by the power of sin he falls into despair and hatred of God or descends into hell, as the Scripture says" (quoted in James Arne Nestingen, "The Catechism's *Simul*," *Word & World* 3 [Fall 1983]: 369). Why must the Gospel follow the preaching of the Law for repentance to be brought to its intended purpose?

3. Read 2 Corinthians 7:10. What is the distinction between worldly grief and godly grief?

4. Commenting on the difference between Law and Gospel, Luther says: "Although, moreover, we say that despair is useful, it is not so by virtue of the law, but a teacher. Thus whenever the law is dealt with, the nature and power and effect of the law is dealt with— that which it is able to do by itself. But when the law pretends that it follows or penetrates the gospel: Hear, quiet down, O Law, see lest you jump your fences. You ought to be a teacher, not a robber, you can terrify, but beware, you may not entirely crush as you once did to Cain, Saul, Judas; remember that you are a teacher. Here is your office, not of a devil or robber, but of a teacher. But these things are not by virtue of the law, but of the gospel and the Holy Spirit as interpreter of the law" (quoted in James Arne Nestingen, "The Catechism's *Simul*," *Word & World* 3 [Fall 1983]: 370). In light of Luther's words, how do you understand Walther's claim: "When we preach the Law, it is not to make men saints, but sinners" (Walther, 293)?

5. How is the Gospel portrayed in Luke 4:18–19 and Ephesians 2:14–17?

6. Read Matthew 12:33. How does the imagery of tree and fruit clarify the relationship of works to true repentance?

7. Why is Romans 14:23 so offensive to human thinking?

8. Read John 3:1–8. What does this passage teach us about faith?

9. Why is it necessary to be especially careful in describing the qualities of faith? What is wrong with a statement such as "a Christian is always joyful"?

NOTES

1. Formula of Concord, Epitome V, 7 (K-W, 501).

2. LW 35:355–411.

3. Gerhard Forde, *On Being a Theologian of the Cross* (Grand Rapids: Eerdmans, 1997), 99.

Chapter Nine

THE POWER OF SIN

In the fourteenth place, the Word of God is not rightly divided when the universal corruption of mankind is described in such a manner as to create the impression that even true believers are still under the spell of ruling sins and are sinning purposely.—C. F. W. Walther (Thesis XVIII [Walther, 318])

In the fifteenth place, the Word of God is not rightly divided when the preacher speaks of certain sins as if they are not of a damnable, but of a venial nature.—C. F. W. Walther (Thesis XIX [Walther, 325])

How are we to speak of the ongoing reality of sin in the life of the Christian? This is the question that Walther seeks to address in these two theses. Unlike many of our day who would minimize sin by speaking of victimization and weakness, of moral mistakes and poor choices, Walther realizes that sin damns. Without the forgiveness of sins obtained by the holy life and sacrificial death of Jesus Christ, all of humanity would be under condemnation and bound for hell. Sin is universal. As the old hymn of Lazarus Spengler puts it:

> All mankind fell in Adam's fall,
> One common sin infects us all;

From sire to son the bane descends,
And over all the curse impends.

Through humankind corruption creeps
And them in dreadful bondage keeps;
In guilt they draw the infant breath
And reap its fruits of woe and death.[1]

This sin, inherited from Adam, is universal. No one can claim to be without sin.

If Law and Gospel are to be correctly distinguished, it is essential that the biblical doctrine of sin be set forth rightly. Here Walther cautions against those who in their desire to make plain the power of our sinful depravity speak in such a way as to give the impression that sin is the natural and normal state of affairs for the Christian. Christ did not come to justify sin but sinners. The life of the Christian is a life of death to sin.

This is the point that the apostle Paul makes in Romans 6:12–14: "Let not sin therefore reign in your mortal bodies, to make you obey their passions. Do not present your members to sin as instruments for unrighteousness, but present yourselves to God as those who have been brought from death to life, and your members to God as instruments for righteousness. For sin will have no dominion over you, since you are not under law but under grace." Jesus Christ, not sin, is Lord in the life of the Christian, for Jesus has brought us under His dominion by the blood of His cross. This leads Walther to observe:

> What the apostle actually says in this text is that sin shall not be able to dominate Christians. It is absolutely impossible that a person who is in a state of grace should be ruled by sin. A pilgrim traveling on a lonely road, when attacked by a highway man, escapes from him at the first opportunity. He does not want to be overcome and slain. Christians are pilgrims through this world on their way to heaven. The devil, like a highway robber, assaults them, and they go down before him because of their weakness, not because they meant to go down. To a true Christian his fall

is forgiven because he daily turns to God in daily repentance with tears or at least heartfelt sighings for pardon. If a person allows sin to rule over him, this is a sure sign that he is not a Christian, but a hypocrite, no matter how pious he pretends to be. (Walther, 320)

Those who live under the dominion of sin will face condemnation (1 Corinthians 6:7–11; Romans 8:13–14; Galatians 5:19–21; Ephesians 5:5–6; 1 Peter 2:20–22). The Law is muted when sin is pictured as compatible with faith. It is a false consolation when "some will lull themselves to sleep with the reflection that they are poor and frail human beings, but that they have faith in Jesus Christ,—however, a lip faith" (Walther, 322).

Does this mean that Christians are perfect and without sin? Not at all. Walther cites the Schmalkald Articles:

Therefore it is necessary to know and teach that when holy people—aside from the fact that they still have and feel original sin and also daily repent of and struggle against it—somehow fall into public sin (such as David, who fell into adultery, murder, and blasphemy against God), at that point faith and the Spirit have departed. The Holy Spirit does not allow sin to rule and gain the upper hand so that it is brought to completion, but the Spirit controls and resists so that sin is not able to do whatever it wants. However, when sin does whatever it wants, then the Holy Spirit and faith are not there. As St. John says (1 John 3:9): "Those who have been born of God do not sin . . . and cannot sin." Nevertheless, this is also the truth (as the same St. John writes [1:8]): "If we say we have no sin, we deceive ourselves, and the truth of God is not in us."[2]

Sin remains, but its dominion has been broken in those who live by faith in Jesus Christ.

Walther is especially adamant in making this point over against the Calvinists who argue that when justified sinners commit mortal sins, they remain in a state of grace and cannot forfeit the Holy Spirit. Such a teaching minimizes the terrible power of sin and confirms sinners in a carnal security and attitude of presumption.

In Thesis XIX, Walther takes up yet another way in which the power of sin is underestimated. This confusion of Law and Gospel misuses the ancient distinction between mortal and venial sins as a way of excusing rather than forgiving sins. According to traditional Roman Catholic teaching, mortal sins (sins such as apostasy, murder, adultery) were so serious as to cut a person off from grace and merit excommunication. Venial sins, on the other hand, were those that did not merit exclusion from the church. Luther would continue to use the distinction between venial and mortal sins—though in a radical way—at the time of the Reformation. This can be seen in the seventh of the Heidelberg Theses (1518) where Luther says, "The works of the righteous would be mortal sins if they would not be feared as mortal sins by the righteous themselves out of pious fear of God."[3] In this way, Luther seeks to undercut every attempt that the sinner would make to find some ground of confidence in his or her good works.

Every sin—both mortal and venial—is to be recognized for what it is: sin. Walther warns that

> we must be scrupulously careful not to create the notion in them [our hearers] that venial sins are sins about which a person need not be greatly concerned and for which he does not have to ask forgiveness . . . . It happens only too often that preachers, when speaking of the distinction between venial and mortal sins, create the impression that to Christians venial sins are matters over which they need not worry. Since all are sinners and no one ever gets rid of sin entirely, there is no reason why one should feel disturbed because of these sins. A talk of that kind is really awful and ungodly. (Walther, 325–26)

Such talk is "awful and ungodly" because it attempts to whittle the Law down to a size that human beings can manage. All religions of the Law operate with the assumption that human beings can accomplish prescribed moral or ceremonial requirements. For example, Islam is highly appealing because it demands no more with its Five Pillars than the average person can achieve. Mormonism is attractive to many because it offers a way of life that is established adherence to clearly defined principles. Such an approach fails to recognize the truth of Jesus' words that not one "dot or iota" (see Matthew 5:18 and James 2:10) will disappear from God's commandments. This Law condemns all sins. It leaves no room for self-defense or self-justification. Again Walther demonstrates his indebtedness to Luther, who asserted that "in the sight of God sins are then truly venial when they are feared to be mortal."[4] This is why a Christian continues to confess himself a "lost and condemned sinner, or all his talk about faith is vain and worthless" (Walther, 328).

The terrible reality of all sin is met with the even greater gift of the Gospel declared by St. John: "[T]he blood of Jesus His Son cleanses us from all sin" (1 John 1:7). However sins may be classified—mortal or venial, great or small—there is forgiveness for all sinners who come with a broken spirit, looking to Christ alone.

FOR REFLECTION AND DISCUSSION

1. What has happened to sin? We often hear the language of evil, victimization, or crime but seldom is the word *sin* used in public discourse. Why is this?

2. "Sin certainly remains as an element in our lives, even though its domination has been broken by the Spirit and faith, recognizing its fearful danger, hates it accordingly" (Adolph Köberle, *The Quest for Holiness*, trans. John C. Mattes [Minneapolis: Augsburg, 1938], 152). How does Romans 6:12–14 help us understand this statement?

3. Read Romans 8:13–14; 1 Corinthians 6:7–11; 1 Peter 2:20–22; Galatians 5:19–21; and Ephesians 5:5–6. What is the common theme in these texts regarding those who live under the lordship of sin?

4. Why is it essential to take 1 John 3:9 and 1 John 1:8 together?

5. What are we told about the nature of the Law in Matthew 5:18–19 and James 2:10?

6. Critique this statement of Charles Finney: "The sinner has all the faculties and natural attributes requisite to render perfect obedience to God. All he needs is to be induced" (Michael Horton, *Made in America: The Shaping of Modern American Evangelicalism* [Grand Rapids: Baker, 1991], 44).

7. Some churches have removed confession and absolution from the worship service, reasoning that it will be experienced as "too negative" because it calls us to acknowledge that we are "poor, miserable sinners." How would such an omission signal a confusion of Law and Gospel?

8. Comment on Walther's statement: "Small sins become great when they are regarded as small" (Walther, 332).

9. Read 1 John 1:7. How inclusive is God's absolution?

NOTES

1. *Lutheran Worship* 363:1–2.
2. Schmalkald Articles III, 3, 43–45 (K-W, 319).
3. LW 31:40.
4. LW 31:40.

Chapter Ten

THE CHURCH:
COMMUNITY OF THE GOSPEL

In the sixteenth place, the Word of God is not rightly divided when a person's salvation is made to depend on his association with the visible orthodox Church and when salvation is denied to every person who errs in any article of faith.—C. F. W. Walther (Thesis XX [Walther, 334])

In the Nicene Creed, we confess "I believe in one holy Christian and apostolic Church." This Christian and apostolic church is an article of faith, not sight. This church is not to be confused with denominational structures or organizations. It is the body of Christ comprised of all those who have faith in the Savior. Of this church, Luther confesses: "God be praised, a seven-year-old child knows what the church is: holy believers and 'the little sheep who hear the voice of their shepherd.' This is why children pray in this way, 'I believe in one holy Christian church.' This holiness does not consist of surplices, tonsures, long albs, or other ceremonies of theirs that they have invented over and above the Holy Scriptures. Its holiness exists in the Word of God and true faith."[1] Reflecting Luther, Walther says the "Church, moreover, is never divided; although its members are separated from one another by space and time, the Church is ever one" (Walther, 337).

There were Lutherans in Walther's day who had forgotten what Luther's seven-year-old knew. In their ardent desire to maintain the truth of the Lutheran confession, they asserted that outside of the "visible church," that is, the Lutheran Church, there is no salvation. Walther rightly identified this error as a confusion of Law and Gospel, for it made salvation dependent not on faith in Jesus Christ alone but on membership in the right organization. It became justification by association, not by faith alone. The key issue for Walther is this: "Making a person's salvation depend on this membership in, and communion with, the visible orthodox Church means to overthrow the doctrine of justification by faith" (Walther, 337).

In addressing this problem, Walther uses the traditional language of the church as "visible" and "invisible." We do well to keep in mind that this terminology can be misunderstood as though there are two churches, one "visible" and the other "invisible." There can be only one church, for there is only one Lord (see Ephesians 4:4–6). Thus the Apology of the Augsburg Confession makes it clear that in speaking about the church we are not "dreaming about some platonic republic."[2] This is why some Lutheran theologians prefer to speak of the church as "hidden" rather than invisible. Hermann Sasse, for example, says: "Hidden under the various church bodies with their different languages and nationalities, constitutions and forms of worship, and other human traditions, lives the one church. Its unity is also hidden under the divisions of Christianity. The one church is purely an article of faith, and yet it is a great reality in the world."[3]

The church lives by God's Word even where that Word is proclaimed along with error. But error never creates faith. Error never builds, but only weakens, the church, but insofar as the truth of the Gospel is proclaimed, the one holy church is there. By the same token, there are unbelievers and false Christians who hold membership in right-teaching congregations.

No one must be induced to join the Lutheran Church because he thinks that only in that way he can get into the Church of God. There are still Christians in the Reformed Church, among the Methodists, yea, among the papists. We have the precious promise in Isaiah 55, 11: "My Word shall not return unto Me void." Wherever the Word of God is proclaimed or confessed or even recited during the service, the Lord is gathering a people for Himself. The Roman Church, for instance, still confesses that Christ is the Son of God and that He died on the cross to redeem the world. That is truth sufficient to bring a man to the knowledge of salvation. Whoever denies this fact is forced to deny also that there are Christians in some Lutheran communities in which errors have cropped out. But there are always some children of God in these communities because they have the Word of God, which is always bearing fruit in converting some souls to God. (Walther, 338).

Doctrinal disease left untreated can lead to spiritual death.

Walther echoes the preface to the *Book of Concord* as he makes the case that our condemnation of false doctrine is not a blanket judgment on Christians who "err in the simplicity of their hearts, but only to obstinate false teachers" (Walther, 340). It is, in fact, for the sake of such Christians that pastors must contend for the truth against false teachers. Every error in doctrine is dangerous. Robert Kolb provides a striking illustration of this point:

Part of what Luther and Melanchthon understood in structuring their confession of faith was that the *articles* or topics of the faith (as found, for example, in the Augsburg Confession) are not so many equally valuable pearls on a string, with so many required to make the string a necklace and so many dispensable. Instead, they believed that Biblical teaching is like a human body. Christ is the head; decapitated it dies. When the arm of Baptism is cut off, or the foot of eschatology badly mangled, the whole body suffers. It can survive with serious injury, but it may also hemorrhage and bleed to death.[4]

The fact that true Christians may be found in false-teaching churches is no excuse for unionism, the practice of church fellowship with those who hold teachings contrary to God's Word. "From the fact that men are saved in all the sects and that in all sectarian churches there are children of God, it by no means follows that one can remain in communion with a sect" (Walther, 339). Church fellowship is not based on the presence of devout Christians but on the pure preaching of God's Word and the right administration of His Sacraments. This biblical teaching is endangered today in a climate that is dominated by doctrinal indifference and a drive toward undiscerning tolerance. Church fellowship is not based on compassion and inclusiveness but on a common confession of God's Word. This is the point made by the Augsburg Confession: "It is also taught that at all times there must be and remain one holy, Christian church. It is the assembly of all believers among whom the gospel is purely preached and the holy sacraments are administered according to the gospel."[5]

The church is not an organization created by human beings. The church belongs to the Lord. This can be seen from any number of New Testament references to the church as the Lord's body, bride, vineyard, flock, temple, and house. The church of Jesus Christ lives from His gifts in sermon and sacrament alone, for through these gifts the Lord creates and sustains faith (see Acts 2:41–42). Nothing that our Lord gives us may be dismissed or set aside (see Matthew 28:20).

Doctrinal indifference flourishes in our pluralistic age where all claims to absolute truth are questioned except the claim that there is no absolute truth. As faith is made subjective so is the practice of church fellowship. Rejection of God's truth is defended on the basis of Christian love. The fact that there are true Christians in heterodox churches may not be used to justify or foster an attitude that accommodates denials of Christ and His Scriptures.

The Lord knows those who are His. This will be revealed on the Last Day. In the meantime we walk by faith, holding to the

Lord's gifts as He gives them. It is only in these holy gifts that we have fellowship with our Lord and with one another in His church.

FOR REFLECTION AND DISCUSSION

1. List some current examples of attempting to make the church something that can be apprehended by sight rather than by faith.

2. Read Ephesians 2:19–22. How does Paul describe the church and our life in the church in this text?

3. What does Paul teach us about the unity of the church in Ephesians 4:4–6? .

4. What does Matthew 28:20 teach us about the basis for church fellowship? How is this fellowship practiced? See Acts 2:41–42; Romans 16:17; and 1 Corinthians 10:16–21.

5. Reflect on these words from Luther and their implication for the church today: "Therefore, as I often warn you, doctrine must be carefully distinguished from life. Doctrine is heaven; life is earth. In life there is sin, error, uncleanness, and misery, mixed, as the saying goes 'with vinegar.' Here love should condone, tolerate, be deceived, trust, hope, and endure all things (1 Cor. 13:7); here the forgiveness of sins should have complete sway, provided sin and error are not defended. But just as there is no error in doctrine, so there is no need for any forgiveness of sins. Therefore there is no comparison at all between doctrine and life. 'One dot' of doctrine is worth more than 'heaven and earth' (Matt. 5:18); therefore we do not permit the slightest offense against it. But we can be lenient in errors of life. For we, too, err daily in our life and conduct; so do all the saints, as they earnestly confess in the Lord's Prayer and the Creed. But by the grace of God our doctrine is pure; we have all the articles of faith established in Sacred Scripture. The devil would dearly love to corrupt and overthrow these; that is why he attacks us so cleverly with this specious argument about not offending against love and the harmony among the churches" (LW 27:41–42). Why is church fellowship a matter of the Gospel?

NOTES

1. Schmalkald Articles III, 12, 2–3 (K-W, 324–25).

2. Apology of the Augsburg Confession VII–VIII, 20 (K-W, 177).

3. Hermann Sasse, *We Confess the Church*, trans. Norman Nagel (St. Louis: Concordia, 1986), 53.

4. Robert Kolb, *Confessing the Faith: Reformers Define the Church 1530–1580* (St. Louis: Concordia, 1991), 136.

5. Augsburg Confession VII, 1 (K-W, 42).

Chapter Eleven

EVANGELICAL SACRAMENTS: FAITH, NOT RITUAL WORKS

In the seventeenth place, the Word of God is not rightly divided when men are taught that the Sacraments produce salutary effects *ex opere operato*, that is, by the mere outward performance of a sacramental act.—C. F. W. Walther (Thesis XXI [Walther, 346])

In this thesis, Walther is echoing Article XIII of the Augsburg Confession:

> Concerning the use of sacraments it is taught that the sacraments are instituted not only to be signs by which people may recognize Christians outwardly, but also as signs and testimonies of God's will toward us in order thereby to awaken and strengthen our faith. That is why they also require faith and are rightly used when received in faith for the strengthening of faith.
>
> Rejected, therefore, are those who teach that the sacraments justify *ex opere operato* without faith and who do not teach that this faith should be added so that the forgiveness of sin (which is obtained through faith and not through work) may be offered there.[1]

Faith does not "make" Baptism and the Lord's Supper, but it is by faith alone that sinners receive the gifts promised and bestowed in these sacraments. Walther, like the Augsburg Confession, takes aim at the old Roman Catholic theory *ex opere operato* (lit., "by the work working"). According to this teaching, the sacraments are beneficial to those who receive them by virtue of "the doing of the act." This turns the gift into a performance that merits grace—a work of human beings rather than the work of the Lord.

> If I am justified, if I obtain grace by my act of going to Communion, I am justified by works, and that, altogether paltry works, scarcely worth mentioning. For that is what Baptism and Holy Communion are when viewed as works that we perform. It is a horrible doctrine, wholly contradicting the Bible, that divine grace is obtained if a person at least makes external use of the Sacraments. (Walther, 346)

Far from being human rituals of washing and eating used to secure standing before God, the Sacraments are God's own instruments established by His words of promise to deliver the forgiveness of sins to all who receive God's gift in faith. When Lutheran pastors urge broken sinners to take comfort in Baptism, they are doing nothing other than urging them to take refuge in Jesus Christ. "To say to a person: 'You must take comfort in your Baptism' and: 'You must turn to Jesus Christ' is identical" (Walther, 348).

"At our baptism it is not we who are performing a work, but God" (Walther, 352). This is crucial in understanding Holy Baptism. Those who see Baptism as simply a churchly custom or an "ordinance" to be fulfilled in obedience to the Lord's command miss the point that Baptism is God's work. Our Lord makes it clear that Baptism is God's work in His conversation with Nicodemus (see John 3:1–8). Here Jesus says, "Truly, truly, I say to you, unless one is born of water and the Spirit, he cannot enter the kingdom of God" (John 3:5). The very imagery of birth demonstrates that Baptism is not something we do any more than we gave ourselves birth. No one gives birth to himself or wills his own birth. The biblical language of rebirth or regeneration (see also 1 Peter 1:3; Titus 3:5–8) indicates that Baptism is the Lord's work.

This is why Peter declares that Baptism "now saves you" (1 Peter 2:21). This same apostle bids his hearers on the day of Pentecost: "Repent and be baptized everyone of you in the name of Jesus Christ for the forgiveness of your sins, and you will receive the gift of the Holy Spirit" (Acts 2:38). This is the promise of Baptism, to be received by faith alone.

Baptism saves because it joins us to the death of Jesus (see Romans 6:3–11). Note how Luther follows the Scriptures in tying Christ's death, Baptism, and faith together:

> Thus you see plainly that baptism is not a work that we do but that it is a treasure that God gives us and faith grasps, just as the LORD Christ upon the cross is not a work but a treasure placed in the setting of the Word and offered to us in the Word and received by faith. Therefore, those who cry out against us as if we were preaching against faith do commit violence against us. Actually, we insist on faith alone as so necessary that without it nothing can be received or enjoyed . . . . In baptism, therefore, every Christian has enough to study and practice all his or her life. Christians always have enough to do to believe firmly what baptism promises and brings—victory over death and the devil, forgiveness of sin, God's grace, the entire Christ, and the Holy Spirit with his gifts.[2]

Faith alone lays hold of the promise made by the Lord in this Sacrament, for Baptism "works forgiveness of sins, delivers from death and the devil, and gives eternal salvation to all who believe, as the words and promises of God declare" (Walther, 354).

Like Luther before him, Walther is engaged in a battle on two fronts. On one hand, he contends against Rome with its false view that faith is not necessary to receive the benefits of the Sacraments. On the other hand, he battles against those Protestants of various stripes who would empty the Sacraments of the efficacy of God's Word. The Lord's Supper, like Baptism, is not a human ceremony that has its power in its performance. It is, the *Lord's* Supper, not the festive celebration of a man-made meal. The words of Jesus (Matthew 26:26–29; Mark 14:22–25; Luke 22:17–20; 1 Corinthians 11:23–25) tell us what this Sacrament is and what the Lord gives in it.

These words of our Lord are the Gospel in a nutshell, for by them He gives us the fruits of His redeeming death on the cross— His body and blood. Salvation was accomplished once and for all by the atoning death of Jesus. Now that redemption is delivered to us in Word and Sacrament. Again recall Luther's words: "If now I seek the forgiveness of sins, I do not run to the cross, for I will not find it there. Nor must I hold to the suffering of Christ, as Dr. Karlstadt trifles, in knowledge or remembrance, for I will not find it there either. But I will find in the sacrament or gospel the word which distributes, presents, offers, and gives me the forgiveness won on the cross."[3]

Under the bread and wine, we are given the very body and blood of the Lord Jesus Christ to eat and to drink. The Sacrament of the Altar is not a representation of Christ's sacrifice. This is no symbolic object lesson pointing back to Good Friday. Neither is the Lord's Supper a ritual drama that relives the Upper Room. It is as the words of Christ declare: His body and blood, given and shed for the forgiveness of sins.

The forgiveness of sins is the primary gift in the Sacrament. The forgiveness of sins is the foundation for the life and salvation that we are given in Jesus' body and blood. Forgiveness of sins is the content of the New Testament. The word *testament* indicates that a death is necessary. The death of the one who makes the testament is necessary for the testament to take effect (see Hebrews 9:18–22). That death occurred on Good Friday. Now we receive the inheritance that our Lord has indicated is ours when He named us as heirs in testamentary words "given and shed for you."

The only salutary way of eating and drinking the Sacrament is in faith. We see this from Paul's example of the unbelieving children of Israel who were judged by God in the wilderness despite the fact that they were baptized into Moses and ate and drank the same spiritual food (see 1 Corinthians 10:1–11). Those who eat and drink the Sacrament without faith eat and drink the very body and blood of Christ in judgment (see 1 Corinthians 11:27–29). But the focus is not on our faith *per se*, as though our faith constitutes the Sacrament. Faith only receives what the Lord gives. The Formula of Concord gives the wise and pastoral advice that "we believe, teach, and confess that no genuine believers—no matter how weak—as long as they retain a living faith, receive the Holy Supper as condemnation. For Christ instituted this supper particularly for Christians who are weak in faith but repentant, to comfort them and to strengthen their weak faith."[4]

It is not the bodily eating and drinking that accomplishes the forgiveness of sins, as the Small Catechism reminds us, "but rather the words that are recorded: 'given for you' and 'shed for you for the forgiveness of sins.' These words, when accompanied by the physical eating and drinking, are the essential thing in the sacrament, and whoever believes these very words has what they declare and state, namely, 'forgiveness of sins' "[5]

Faith receives all that the Lord gives in the ways that He gives it—the reading and preaching of the Scriptures, Holy Baptism, Holy Absolution, and the Sacrament of the Altar are all from Him. Through these, the Lord gives and bestows the forgiveness of sins and with His forgiveness, all the riches of His grace—life with Him now and the promise of eternal salvation. There is only one way to receive Jesus' gifts—by faith.

FOR REFLECTION AND DISCUSSION

1. Discuss the statement: "Faith does not make the Sacrament but receives the Sacrament."

2. How does Walther see Law and Gospel being confused in the misuse of the Sacraments?

3. In what sense are the statements "We are saved by Jesus Christ" and "Baptism now saves you" identical? See 1 Peter 3:21.

4. Read John 3:1–8. How does Jesus illustrate that Baptism is God's work?

5. Read Matthew 26:26–27. What is the gift of the Lord's Supper?

6. How does the apostle Paul connect faith and the Sacrament of the Altar in 1 Corinthians 10:1–11 and 11:27–29?

7. Reflect on these words from the Formula of Concord in light of the distinction between Law and Gospel: "The true and worthy guests, for whom this precious sacrament above all was instituted and established, are the Christians who are weak in faith, fragile and troubled, who are terrified in their hearts by the immensity and number of their sins and think that they are not worthy of this precious treasure and the benefits of Christ because of their great impurity, who feel the weakness of their faith and deplore it, and who desire to serve God with a stronger, more resolute faith and purer obedience . . . . Moreover, this worthiness consists not in a greater or lesser weakness or strength of faith, but rather in the merit of Christ, which the troubled father with his weak faith (Mark 9:24) possessed, just as did Abraham, Paul, and others who have a resolute, strong faith" (Solid Declaration VII, 69–71 [K-W, 605–6]).

NOTES

1. Augsburg Confession XIII, 1–3 (K-W, 46).

2. Large Catechism, "Baptism," 37, 41 (K-W, 461).

3. LW 40:214.

4. Formula of Concord, Epitome VII, 19 (K-W, 506).

5. Small Catechism, "The Sacrament of the Altar," 8 (K-W, 363).

Chapter Twelve

ALIVE BY THE GOSPEL

In the eighteenth place, the Word of God is not rightly divided when a false distinction is made between a person's being awakened and his being converted; moreover, when a person's INABILITY to believe is mistaken for his not BEING PERMITTED to believe.—C. F. W. Walther (Thesis XXII [Walther, 362] *Walther's emphasis*)

In the twentieth place, the Word of God is not rightly divided when the unforgivable sin against the Holy Ghost is described in a manner as if it could not be forgiven because of its magnitude.—C. F. W. Walther (Thesis XXIV [Walther, 393])

The Gospel of Jesus Christ makes alive. The opposite of life is death. One is either alive or dead. There is no third option, no territory between life and death. Just so there is only unbelief or faith. One is either converted to faith in Jesus Christ and has life in His name or a person remains unconverted and, therefore, dead in his sins. "According to Scripture we can assume only two classes: those who are converted and those who are not" (Walther, 363).

Here Walther is taking aim at the false distinction made by the Pietists between being "awakened" and being "converted." The Pietist movement emerged in the last part of the seventeenth century in Germany. While on the surface it might appear that this movement was a reaction to certain perceived weaknesses in traditional Lutheranism, in fact, the Pietists represented a new theology that had shifted away from the objectivity of the means of grace to the subjectivity of the interior life of the Christian. Emphasis was placed on the quality of the human response to the Gospel in individual piety, worship, and behavior.[1] Pietism is seen today, even in confessional Lutheran churches, in approaches to worship, evangelism, and church life that focus on emotion and response rather than on the pure preaching of the Gospel.

According to the Pietists, there are three classes within humanity: unconverted sinners, awakened sinners who have not yet been converted, and those who have been converted. But the Bible teaches that salvation never comes in bits and pieces. God does not deal with us in fractions. The Pietists erred in thinking that sinners come to Christ in stages and through their own anguished struggles. No matter how weak his faith may be, the person who trusts Jesus Christ is a new creation (1 Corinthians 5:17) and has life in His name. To treat such a person as an unbeliever throws him back on his own efforts to find assurance in himself. It robs him of the peace that Christ promises in the Gospel. Feelings do not guarantee faith. In fact, emotions are completely unreliable when it comes to the Word of God. Our emotions too easily distort both God's Law and Gospel, deceiving us and leading into deeper despair. There is only one cure for the heart crushed by the Law, and it is not a rigorous regimen of agonized self-improvement. It is the Gospel of the Lord Jesus—Jesus who gives life to the dead.

Conflict will come, but it is not a conflict that leads to conversion. This conflict is that of trial and cross bearing, of doing battle against the devil, the world, and the flesh. Where the Gospel produces faith, there will be conflict. This conflict is not a stage on the road to conversion but a characteristic of the ongoing life of repentance and faith.

The Calvinistic teaching of double predestination is another way that troubled consciences are seduced into despair. According to this doctrine, God from eternity elected some to salvation and others to damnation. His arbitrary, sovereign decree results in faith for some and unbelief for others, according to classical Reformed theology. Reformed theology fits well with human reason, for it begins with the power of God, His sovereign rule, and His awesome majesty. Here God's almighty nature is key. He can do as He pleases. He can predestine some to perdition and others to paradise because He has that power. While Lutherans also confess that God is almighty, Lutheran theology does not begin with His majesty but with His mercy in Christ. The Law shows us the sovereignty of God and His power over sinners, but the Gospel alone delivers the mercy of God in the blood of Jesus Christ.

Lutherans confess the doctrine of election as it is biblically defined (see Ephesians 1:3–14 and Romans 8:28–30). On the basis of Holy Scriptures, the Formula of Concord confesses that eternal election ought not "be conceived of as a military muster, in which God said, 'this one shall be saved, that one shall be damned; this one will remain faithful, that one will not remain faithful.' "[2] Instead, this doctrine provides profound comfort for Christians who live under crosses and trials. Law and Gospel are blurred by this fatalistic misuse of the doctrine of election. It equates the inability to believe with the thought that God does not permit some to believe. Werner Elert aptly gets to the point when he says that "peace of conscience, which is the important matter here, is not the false security of synergism-just as it should not be the false security of a fatalistic belief in salvation."[3]

God works faith through the Gospel. This Gospel is the good news that God was in Christ reconciling the world to Himself (see 2 Corinthians 5:18–21). The death that Jesus Christ died on the cross was atonement for the sin of the whole world. Paul writes that since "one has died for all, therefore all have died; and He died for all, that those who live might no longer live for themselves but for Him who died for their sake and was raised" (2 Corinthians

5:14–15). "By this precious statement the apostle means to say that, since Christ died, it is the same as if all men had suffered death for their sins, namely, the death which Christ died; it is the same as if all had atoned for their sins by their death. Now that the entire world has been redeemed and reconciled to God, is it not a horrible teaching to tell any person he may not believe that he has been reconciled and redeemed and has the forgiveness of sins?" (Walther, 374). The universal reconciliation accomplished by Jesus on the cross is the basis for the preaching of forgiveness. Without His death for the sins of the whole world, absolution would be empty.

Redemption has been accomplished in the blood of Jesus shed on the cross. Now it is to be distributed in sermon and Sacrament. Baptism, the Lord's Supper, the word of absolution, preaching, and every speaking of the Gospel is a delivery of the fruits of Calvary. Broken sinners are not left to struggle their way into God's kingdom. Nor are they left to speculate whether or not they are among the elect. God's pardon on account of Christ's death is sure and certain.

> By the resurrection of Christ, God has declared that He is reconciled with all mankind and does not intend to inflict punishment on anybody. He has this fact proclaimed in all the world by His Gospel and, in addition, has commanded every minister of the Gospel to forgive men their sins, promising that He will do in heaven what the minister is doing on earth. The minister is not first to look up to heaven to ascertain what God is doing; he is merely to execute His orders on earth and forgive people's sins, relying on God's promises that He is forgiving them. (Walther, 375–76)

This is why Luther continually urges those troubled by unanswerable questions regarding election to cease their incessant speculation and rely on Christ crucified as He gives us His sure promises in the means of grace. In one of his Table Talks, Luther says that we are to avoid prying into the mystery of election, for such internal disputation "is like a fire that cannot be extinguished."[4] Instead, Luther counters, "Our Lord God is so hostile to such disputation that he instituted Baptism, the Word, and the Sacraments to counteract it."[5] Faith sticks with what Christ gives.

If Christ died for all sins, how are we to understand the sin or the blasphemy against the Holy Spirit that Jesus says will not be forgiven? Using Matthew 12:30–32 as his key text, Walther says:

> It states, to begin with, that all blasphemy against the Father and the Son shall be forgiven. . . . Now, it is certain that the Holy Spirit is not a more glorious and exalted person than the Father and the Son, but He is coequal with them. Accordingly, the meaning of this passage cannot be that the unforgivable sin is blasphemy against the person of the Holy Spirit; for blasphemy against the Father and the Son is exactly the same sin. The blasphemy to which our text refers is directed *against the office,* or operation, of the Holy Spirit; whoever spurns the office of the Holy Spirit, his sin cannot be forgiven. The office of the Holy Spirit is to call men to Christ and to keep them with Him. (Walther, 393, *Walther's emphasis*)

To sin against the Holy Spirit is to refuse the Gospel that He causes to be preached. It is the sin of utter and ultimate unbelief. It is the obstinate and willful rejection of the very means that the Holy Spirit uses to create faith. Paul clarifies this as he writes: "Therefore I want you to understand that no one speaking in the Spirit of God ever says 'Jesus is accursed!' and no one can say 'Jesus is Lord' except in the Holy Spirit" (1 Corinthians 12:3).

Walther points out that the sin against the Holy Spirit is unforgivable not because it is too great for Calvary but because the person who commits this sin refuses the gift of forgiveness of sins: "The sin is not unpardonable because of its magnitude—for the apostle, as we heard has distinctly declared: 'Where sin abounded, grace did much more abound'—but because the person committing this sin rejects the only means by which he can be brought to repentance, faith, and steadfastness in faith" (Walther, 397–98). Final impenitence is a characteristic of this sin. For that reason, it is impossible to restore such a person (see Hebrews 6:4–8). It is, as the apostle John says, a "sin unto death" (see 1 John 5:16), for it forever refuses the life that Christ alone gives.

Paul was a blasphemer of Christ (see 1 Timothy 1:13). Stephen prays for those who stone him, imploring the Lord to forgive them for resisting the Holy Spirit (see Acts 7:51–60). In this life, we should not despair of any person or conclude that he is beyond the reach of the Gospel. Rather, with patience and prayer we continue to hold out to them the Word of Life who alone is able to rescue them from condemnation.

Sometimes Christians are vexed with evil thoughts that lead them to worry that they have committed the unforgivable sin. Here Walther offers excellent pastoral advice.

> As regards people who are distressed because they think that they have committed the sin against the Holy Ghost, they would not feel distressed if they had really committed that sin and were in that awful condition of heart, but they would find their constant delight in blaspheming the Gospel. However, Christians in distress still have faith, and the Spirit of God is working in them; and if the Spirit of God is working in them, they have not committed the sin against the Holy Ghost. (Walther, 399)

The sin against the Holy Spirit is unforgivable because it rejects the forgiveness that Jesus Christ offers. Troubled consciences terrified by Satan's tactics find rest and peace in a Savior whose forgiveness was deep enough to forgive a denier like Peter and a persecutor like Paul. No sin is too big for Calvary, and no sinner is beyond the embrace of Jesus Christ. Those who will not receive the gifts of Christ Jesus are left in their sin and under condemnation not because their sin is too great to be forgiven but because they will not trust in this forgiveness.

FOR REFLECTION AND DISCUSSION

1. Read Ephesians 2:4–6; Ephesians 5:14; and Colossians 2:11–14. How do these texts support Walther's assertion that there are only two classes of people spiritually?

2. How is the Gospel distorted by the notion that there are three categories of human beings—the unconverted, the awakened, and the converted?

3. What evidences of Pietism do you see in contemporary church life? What are the spiritual dangers of Pietism?

4. The Formula of Concord sees the doctrine of election as part of the Gospel. "This doctrine also gives us wonderful comfort in crosses and trials, that in his counsel before time began God determined and decreed that he would stand by us in every trouble, grant us patience, give us comfort, create hope, and provide a way out of all things so that we may be saved (cf. I Cor. 10:13" (Solid Declaration XI, 48 [K-W, 648]). See also Ephesians 1:3–14 and Romans 8:28–30. How does Walther use this doctrine evangelically, that is, according to the Gospel?

5. Read 2 Corinthians 5:14–15, 18–21. What is the scope of Christ's atonement? How is universal atonement the basis for the speaking of absolution? How does synergism (the belief that man cooperates with God in his salvation) give a false security?

6. Read Matthew 12:30–32. What is the blasphemy against the Holy Spirit? Why is this sin unforgivable? Also see 1 Corinthians 12:3 and Luther's explanation of the Third Article of the Creed in the Small Catechism.

NOTES

1. For a good overview of Pietism, see Bengt Hagglund, *History of Theology*, trans. Gene Lund (St. Louis: Concordia, 1968), 325–34.

2. Formula of Concord, Solid Declaration XI, 9 (K-W, 642).

3. Werner Elert, *The Structure of Lutheranism*, trans. Walter Hansen (St. Louis: Concordia, 1962), 130.

4. Theodore Tappert, comp., *Luther: Letters of Spiritual Counsel* (Louisville: Westminster/John Knox, 1955), 122.

5. Tappert, *Luther: Letters of Spiritual Counsel*, 122.

Chapter Thirteen

THE GOSPEL GETS THE LAST WORD

In the nineteenth place, the Word of God is not rightly divided when an attempt is made, by means of the demands or the threats of the promises of the Law, to induce the unregenerate to put away their sins and engage in good works and thus become godly; on the other hand, when an endeavor is made, by means of the commands of the Law rather than by the admonitions of the Gospel, to urge the regenerate to do good.—C. F. W. Walther (Thesis XXIII [Walther, 381])

In the twenty–first place, the Word of God is not rightly divided when the person teaching it does not allow the Gospel to have a general predominance in his teaching.— C. F. W. Walther (Thesis XXV [Walther, 403])

Walther goes right to the jugular vein of much "pop" Christianity when he says, "The attempt to make men godly by means of the Law and to induce even those who are already believers in Christ to do good by holding up the Law and issuing commands to them, is a very gross confounding of Law and Gospel" (Walther, 381). Yet this is just what we see in contemporary spirituality. For example, Rick Warren, in his best-selling book *The Purpose-Driven Life,* holds before his readers the promise that their lives will have less stress, increased satisfaction, simplified decisions, and will be prepared for eternity if they follow his forty-day pattern of biblical directives. The commands of the Law are held up to urge Christians to perform. The focus is off of the Gospel and on our ability to reshape our attitudes and behavior.

The Law of God is "good and wise" go the words of an old hymn. That same hymn continues

> The Law is good; but since the fall
> Its holiness condemns us all;
> It dooms us for our sin to die
> And has no pow'r to justify.[1]

Luther made the astounding discovery that "The law of God, the most salutary doctrine of life, cannot advance humans on their way to righteousness, but rather hinders them."[2] The Law paints the portrait of the life of goodness and blessing, but it is absolutely powerless to create and bestow this life. Walther says:

> How foolish, then, is a preacher who thinks that conditions in his congregation will improve if he thunders at his people with the Law and paints hell and damnation for them. That will not at all improve the people. Indeed, there is a time for such preaching of the Law in order to alarm secure sinners and make them contrite, but a change of heart and love of god and one's fellow-men is not produced by the Law. (Walther, 384–85)

When the Law is preached to the unregenerate in an attempt to make them godly, it actually has the opposite effect. When the Law is mishandled in this way, it results in frustration and deepened defiance of God in the hearer, or it seduces the hearer into a false security that once sinful behaviors are under control one is right with God. Gerhard Forde describes this as being "addicted either to what is base or to what is high, either to lawlessness or to lawfulness."[3] The end result is the same because in both cases God is not trusted as the Savior. Self-righteousness is simply another form of unrighteousness, for "by works of the law no human being will be justified in His sight, since through the law comes knowledge of sin" (Romans 3:20).

It is the Gospel, not the Law, that gives birth to the new life of faith. The Gospel alone enlivens believers for the life of good works. Yes, the Law must continue to be proclaimed to Christians, for we are simultaneously saints and sinners. Christians need the Law to guard them from falling back on "their own holiness and piety and under the appearance of God's Spirit establish their own service to God on the basis of their own choice."[4] But the Christian life is not a product of the Law. As the old Adam stubbornly clings to the new man, the Law is still needed to put him back where he belongs—in the watery grave of Baptism. So the Formula of Concord says:

> For the old creature, like a stubborn, recalcitrant donkey, is also still a part of them, and it needs to be forced into obedience to Christ not only through the law's teaching, admonition, compulsion, and threat but also often with the cudgel of punishments and tribulations until the shameful flesh is completely stripped away and people are perfectly renewed in the resurrection. Then they will need neither the proclamation of the law nor its threats and punishment, just as they will no longer need the gospel, for both belong to this imperfect life. Instead, just as they will see God face-to-face, so they will perform the will of God by the power of the indwelling Spirit of God spontaneously, without coercion, unhindered, perfectly and completely, with sheer joy, and they will delight in his will eternally.[5]

Sanctification comes not from the power of the Law but from the living words of the Gospel, words that take root in the heart and produce good fruits on the lips and in the lives of those who through faith are righteous. These good works are not trophies of personal achievement or bargaining chips with the Almighty. They are fruits of faith and are directed to the neighbor in his or her need. So Walther counsels future pastors:

> Let no minister think that he cannot induce the unwilling to do God's will by preaching the Gospel to them and that

he must rather preach the Law and proclaim the threatenings of God to them. If that is all he can do, he will only lead his people to perdition. Rather than act the policemen in his congregation, he ought to change the hearts of his members in order that they may without constraints do what is pleasing to God with a glad and cheerful heart. A person who has a real understanding of the love of God in Christ Jesus is astonished at its fire, which is able to melt anything in heaven and on earth. The moment he believes in this love he cannot but love God and from this gratitude for his salvation do anything from love of God and His glory. It is a useless effort to try to soften with laws and threatenings such hearts as are not melted by having the love of God in Christ Jesus presented to them. The best preachers are those who in this respect do as Luther did, such as preach the Law only accomplish nothing. In such measures as you exhibit the Law in its spiritual meaning, in that measure you sink your hearers into despair, but do not make them willing to serve God. (Walther, 389)

Fearing, loving, and trusting God above all things cannot be accomplished by the coercion of the Law. Only the words of the Gospel written in the heart with the blood of God's own Son can free from sin and create a new man who lives in righteousness and holiness forever. Where the Gospel reigns through faith in Jesus Christ, there is a new life lived not by the threats of the Law but in freedom. Christian freedom is liberty *from* sin, not *for* sin. It is the freedom for life in Christ, a life that is now liberated to give oneself in loving service to the neighbor.

This is a freedom that comes only in Christ. Bound to Christ, we are free from the self. Luther described it like this in his tract on "The Freedom of the Christian": "We conclude, therefore, that a Christian lives not in himself, but in Christ and in his neighbor. Otherwise he is not a Christian. He lives in Christ through faith, in his neighbor through love."[6] Six years later, Luther would give this thought liturgical expression in the post-Communion collect in which he prays that the salutary gift of Jesus' body and blood would strengthen us in faith toward God and fervent love toward one another. It is the Gospel, not the Law, that frees and enlivens Christians for works of love directed at the neighbor's needs.

Walther's final thesis brings his whole argument to culmination. When Law and Gospel are rightly divided, the Gospel comes out on top. The Law must be spoken to diagnose the sin and expose as quackery every remedy the sinner would devise to mitigate the disease. But the Law always stands in service of the Gospel; it is always subordinate to the Gospel. The Gospel alone can provide healing for the wounds uncovered by the Law. Troubled people with consciences torn by sin and hearts distressed by doubt will find no rest or peace in the Law. Walther cites the Christmas angel as the model for all genuinely evangelical preaching because this heavenly messenger comes not with the thundering words of Law but a Gospel-filled greeting: "Fear not, for behold, I bring you good news of a great joy that will be for all people. For unto you is born this day in the city of David a Savior, who is Christ the Lord" (Luke 2:10–11). "This heavenly preacher gave us an illustration of how we are to preach. True, we have to preach the Law, only, however, as a preparation for the Gospel. The ultimate aim in our preaching of the Law must be to preach the Gospel. Whoever does not adopt this aim is not a true minister of the Gospel" (Walther, 404). The Gospel magnifies the merits of Christ and extols His work of redemption. The Law is all about human beings, our sin, our failure, and ultimately our death. The Gospel is all about Christ Jesus, His righteousness, His faithfulness, and His atoning death. Because it is about us, the Law brings terror. Because it is of Christ, the Gospel brings God's own consolation and calms the terrified conscience.

Jesus' atoning death on the cross has removed the curse of sin from the whole world. God's wrath is absorbed in the blood of Christ. Only unbelief damns. Referencing Mark 16:15–16 ("Whoever believes and is baptized will be saved, but whoever does not believe will be condemned"), Walther says: "No matter what a person's character is and how grievously he has sinned, nothing in his past record shall damn him. But, naturally, when a person refuses to believe the words, the message, of Jesus, he has to go to perdition. The Lord never makes mention of hell except for the purpose of bringing men to heaven" (Walther, 404).

The good news that Jesus is the friend of sinners, the one who justifies the godless, is the source of joy. When pastors preach the pure Gospel of Jesus Christ without diluting it with human works, they are "helpers of the Christians' joy" (Walther, 407). Such joy is not the shallow thrill of momentary excitement but the bedrock confidence of sins forgiven and peace with God restored. The preaching of the Gospel chases away all gloomy thoughts with the announcement that the crucified and risen Lord has taken sin captive and robbed death of its sting. This is not a counterfeit gospel of carnal security that makes peace with sin; it is a word from the lips of Christ that delivers both pardon and liberation. Walther quotes Luther:

> By His ascension and by the preaching of faith, Christ does not purpose to rear lazy Christians, who say: We shall now live according to our own pleasure, not doing good works, remaining sinners, and following sin like captive slaves. *Those who talk thus have never had a right understanding of the preaching of faith.* Christ and His mercy are not preached to the end that men should remain in their sins. On the contrary, this is what the Christian doctrine proclaims: The captivity is to leave you go free, not that you may do whatever you desire, but that you sin no more. (Walther, 411, *Walther's emphasis*)

We are never to hesitate speaking the Gospel fully, purely, and freely for the fear that this precious message might be abused. We are, Walther says, "to preach the real Gospel with its comfort without hesitation and not fear that we shall preach people into hell with the Gospel" (Walther, 411). True, some may misuse this divine Word, using it as a justification for their sins. But such carnal security is a fleshly deception that cannot endure the challenge of death.

Only the Gospel can produce faith and that is why Walther is so insistent that it predominates Christian preaching, even if there are those who distort its declaration of freedom from sin to freedom for sin. We are tempted to make the Gospel conditional on something in our thinking or doing. But that leaves us back in bondage. In that slavery there is only death and condemnation. But where the Gospel shines, there is the radiant light of Easter's new day, of freedom from sin and death, of an open heaven and a locked-up hell. God gets the last word, and in His Son it is the word of the Gospel, for "all the promises of God find their Yes in Him" (2 Corinthians 1:20). So we are bold to pray:

> Almighty God, grant to your Church your Holy Spirit and the wisdom which comes down from heaven that your Word may not be bound but have free course and be preached to the joy and edifying of Christ's holy people, that in steadfast faith we may serve you and in the confession of your name may abide to the end; through Jesus Christ, our Lord.[7]

FOR REFLECTION AND DISCUSSION

1. Study the hymn "The Law of God Is Good and Wise" (*Lutheran Worship* 329) in light of 1 Timothy 1:8–11. How is "the law good, if one uses it lawfully" (1 Timothy 1:8)?

2. Why is it tempting to rely on the Law rather than the Gospel in living the Christian life?

3. What happens when we try to use the Law to accomplish what the Gospel alone can do?

4. What do lawlessness and self–righteousness have in common?

5. Read Jeremiah 31:31–34. Where does Jeremiah say that God has written His Law? What are the implications of this for the Christian life? See also Psalm 119:32.

6. Why is the Law still needed in the life of the Christian? How does the Formula of Concord describe the function of the Law in the life of the Christian? See Formula of Concord, Solid Declaration VI, 20–25 (K-W 590-91).

7. How is Luke 2:10–11 a good example of Gospel proclamation?

8. How is the Law subordinate to the Gospel in Mark 16:15–16?

9. How would you answer the accusation that the preaching of the Gospel creates moral laxity and spiritual laziness?

10. Read Ephesians 3. How does Paul describe the power of the Gospel? What is the nature of this power, and what does it accomplish?

11. Reflect on the post-Communion collect: "We give thanks to you, almighty God, that you have refreshed us through this salutary gift, and we implore you that of your mercy you would strengthen us through the same in faith toward you and fervent love toward one another; through Jesus Christ, your Son, our Lord, who lives and reigns with you and the Holy Spirit, one God, now and forever" (*Lutheran Worship*, p. 153). How does this prayer express the Christian life in the way of the Gospel?

NOTES

1. *Lutheran Worship* 329:5.

2. Gerhard Forde, *On Being a Theologian of the Cross* (Grand Rapids: Eerdmans, 1997), 23.

3. Forde, *On Being a Theologian of the Cross*, 27.

4. Formula of Concord, Solid Declaration VI, 20 (K-W, 590).

5. Formula of Concord, Solid Declaration VI, 24–25 (K-W, 591).

6. LW 31:371.

7. *Lutheran Worship*, p. 243.

Appendix

THE DISTINCTION BETWEEN LAW AND GOSPEL[1]

A SERMON BY MARTIN LUTHER

JANUARY 1, 1532

Gal. 3, 23–24. Now before faith came, we were confined under the law, kept under restraint until faith should be revealed. So that the law was our custodian until Christ came, that we might be justified by faith . . .

1. What St. Paul has in mind is this: That throughout Christendom preachers and hearers alike should teach and should maintain a clear distinction between the Law and the Gospel, between works and faith. He so instructed Timothy, admonishing him (2 Tim. 2:15) to "divide rightly the word of truth." Distinguishing between the Law and the Gospel is the highest art in Christendom, one that every person who values the name Christian ought to recognize, know and possess. Where this is lacking, it is not possible to tell who is Christian and who is pagan or Jew. That much is at stake in this distinction.

2. That is why St. Paul strongly insists that among Christians these two doctrines, the Law and the Gospel, are to be well and truly separated from one another. Both of them are the Word of God: the Law (or the Ten Commandments), and the Gospel. Both were given by God: the Gospel originally in Paradise, the Law on Mt. Sinai. That is why it is so important to distinguish the two words properly and not mingle them together. Otherwise you will not be able to have or hold on to a correct understanding of either of them. Instead, just when you think you have them both, you will have neither.

3. Under the papacy the point was reached where neither the pope himself nor any of his scholars, cardinals, bishops or universities ever knew what either Gospel or Law might be. They never tasted, nor did they let it be known in any of their books, how the one is to be distinguished from the other—how the doctrine of the Law should or could be kept apart from the Gospel. For that reason their faith is, to say the best, purely and simply a Turk's faith which stands solely upon the bare letter of the Law and on outward acts of doing or not doing, such as "You shall not kill" and "You shall not steal." They take the view that the Law is satisfied if a man does not use his fist for homicide, does not steal anyone's property, and the like. In short, they believe that sort of external piety is a righteousness that prevails before God, etc. But such doctrine and faith is false and wrong, even though the works performed are themselves good and have been commanded by God. For the Law demands a righteousness much higher than one based on external virtues and piety; while the Gospel of grace and the forgiveness of sins is totally knocked to the ground by their doctrine. For however much not stealing or not committing homicide is behavior that is right and mandated by the Law, it is still nothing more than a piety of the Gentiles which fails to attain the righteousness demanded by the Law. Far less can it be equated with the forgiveness of sins that the Gospel teaches and proclaims.

4. It is therefore urgent that these two words, different in kind,

be rightly and properly distinguished. Where that is not done, neither the Law nor the Gospel can be understood, and consciences
must perish in blindness and error. For the Law has its terminus,
defining how far it is to go and what it is to achieve: namely, to terrify the impenitent with the wrath and displeasure of God and
drive them to Christ. Likewise the Gospel has its unique office and
function: to preach the forgiveness of sins to troubled consciences.
Let doctrine then not be falsified, either by mingling these two into
one, or by mistaking the one for the other. For the Law and the
Gospel are indeed both God's word; but they are not the same kind
of doctrine. It is like the word of God in Exodus 20:12, "You shall
honor your father and your mother," and the one found in Ephesians 6:4, "You fathers, bring up your children in the training and
instruction of the Lord." Since the two words do not address the
same office or the same persons, what chaos would follow if they
were thrown together on the grounds that "it is all God's Word"!
The son would then want to be father and the father would want to
be the son. Mother would want to be daughter and daughter to be
the mother. But that lacks rhyme or reason and is intolerable. The
father should do what God has assigned and commanded him to
do. Likewise let the son attend to his calling. In this way duties and
functions are properly distinguished and distributed. So too it is fitting for the mother in a family to bear children and nurse them and
bring them up; and for a husband to provide for his household and
servants and manage them faithfully, but not to bear children or
take over the housekeeping, attending, etc. When someone begins
to interfere in the office assigned to another, or tries to take it over
and annex it to his own, what kind of chaos and turmoil does that
not soon produce? The word must be rightly distinguished, so that
each person looks after what he has been called and assigned to do,
stays with it, and goes no farther. That way he will not go astray.

5. It was nothing else than this that brought Thomas Muenzer
into such terrible trouble. He read in the books of the Kings how
David slew the wicked with the sword; how Joshua destroyed the

Canaanites, Hittites, and other godless peoples who were dwelling in the land of Canaan; etc. Finding that word in the Scripture, he drew from it the conclusion that we must all do the same. We must crush kings and ruling princes, because we have this example. But where Muenzer fell short was in failing to distinguish the word correctly. Otherwise he would have said to himself: Yes, David fought wars. But am I David? The word that told David to fight wars is not addressed to me. He received the command to make war and slay kings; I have received the command to preach. Muenzer should have left fighting alone and gone into the pulpit and taught the pure Gospel as Christ commanded: "Go into all the world and preach the Gospel to the whole creation." Had he done that, he would not have gotten into such terrible doctrine and uproar. To David and not to Muenzer it was said: "You shall protect the righteous, smite the wicked with the sword, maintain peace, etc." But if David would neglect those duties and go intruding into the priestly office, and if I would drop preaching and take up the sword, and so mix everything up, what kind of prize government and high art would we not then have? For the barnyard, perhaps.

6. Therefore I say it again: Properly separating the Law and the Gospel from one another is a very high art, since it is necessary to do the same also with the commandments (all of which are included under the one word "Law"). We have to distinguish the one from the other, unless we want everything to be completely and totally mixed up—and because there is still failure and defect even when every right and proper distinction has been made.

7. Hence it is a serious misunderstanding, and indeed foolishness, when somebody pleads: "It is the word of God, it is the word of God, therefore it is right, etc." The Word of God is not all of the same kind; it is of diverse kinds. The Law is a different word from the Gospel. Likewise the laws or commandments are not all of the same kind. The word of God, "Protect the righteous, punish the wicked," does not apply to me. Nor does the word: "Bear children, nurse them, sweep, attend," etc., which applies alone to the women.

Likewise: "Thou shalt preach, thou shalt administer the sacraments," belongs not to female but to male persons who have been called to that office.

8. Our "enthusiasts" know nothing at all of this distinction— neither how to make it, nor what the distinction is in theory or in practice. One law is held up in opposition to another on the grounds that the one is just as much law as the other. When dealing with laws, however, it is necessary to separate them one from another and to pay proper attention to the persons at whom the law is directed. How much more important is it, then, to make a distinction between the Law and the Gospel. Therefore whoever knows well this art of dividing the Law from the Gospel should be given a place at the front of the room and be called a doctor of Holy Scripture. For it is impossible to make this distinction without the Holy Spirit. I experience in myself, and I see every day in others, how hard it is to separate the doctrines of the Law and the Gospel from one another. In this the Holy Spirit has to be the master and teacher, or no person on earth would be able to understand or teach the distinction. Hence no papist, no false Christian, no "enthusiast" is able to divide Law and Gospel from one another, especially when it comes to defining what each of them is.

We should understand "Law" to mean nothing else than God's word and command, in which he directs us what to do and what not to do, and demands from us our obedience or "work." This is easy to understand as a statement of what gives the law its character, but very difficult in terms of its purpose and its limits. The individual laws or commandments, dealing with the works that God requires of all people severally on the basis of what they are, their social position, their office, age, and other circumstances, are of many kinds. They tell every human being what God has laid upon him and requires of him in keeping with his nature and assigned office. The woman shall attend to the children, permit the head of the household to take the lead, etc. That is her commandment. A servant is to be obedient to his master and do whatever else belongs to the office of a servant. Likewise a maid has her directive. The overall law, however, which applies to us all as human beings, is this (Matt. 22:39): "You shall love your neighbor as yourself," counsel and help him in his need, whatever it may be. If he hungers, feed him; if he is naked, clothe him; and whatever else of that sort there is. That means giving the Law its rightful boundaries, and marking it off from the Gospel: the Law, in name and in fact, is that which presses us to do our works.

On the other hand the Gospel or the faith is a doctrine or word of God that does not require our works. It does not command us to do anything. On the contrary it bids us merely to accept the offered grace of forgiveness of sins and eternal life and let it be given to us. It means that we do nothing; only receive, and allow ourselves to be given what has been granted to us and handed to us in the Word: that God promises and allows his servants to tell you, "I am giving you this and this, etc." For example, in Baptism, which is not my doing or my work, but God's Word and work, God speaks to me and says: "Stop right here; I baptize you, I wash you from all your sins; accept it; it is for you." If now you let yourself be baptized, what more are you doing than receiving and accepting God's free gift? So this now is the difference between the Law and the Gospel. The Law presses us to do what we are supposed to do; it demands that we do our duty towards God and our neighbor. In the Gospel on the other hand we are summoned to a gift of alms, to a rich distribution of charity, where we are to receive and accept God's favor and eternal salvation.

9. Hence this difference is easily to be noted. The Gospel bids us come to God's gift and present, to his help and his salvation. We just hold out the beggar's bag and let it be given us. The Law on the other hand gives us nothing; it only demands and takes from us. So now there is this pair, giving and taking, widely separate from one another. When something is given to me as a gift, I do nothing towards it. I accept it and receive it and let it be given to me. Conversely, when I carry out in my calling what I have been com-

manded to do—for example, counsel and help my neighbor—I am not receiving anything, but am giving something to another, whom I serve. In this way the Law and the Gospel are distinguished in their essential character: the one promises, the other commands. The Gospel gives and that means that we receive. The Law issues demands and says: Thou shalt. It is like when a prince or a liege lord presents his property to a nobleman. The nobleman does nothing; it is not his work; it is a bequest by the prince. But when he mounts his horse to serve his lord or to attend him at court, then he is doing something.

10. Hence this pair of doctrines are to be widely divided from one another, but in the Spirit. For the devil, to torment hearts, does not let us remain with what the Law's words say, or with its goal. He does allow it to happen that something is done or performed; but he leads us away from what we were commanded to do to something else allegedly Higher and Better. He does the same sort of thing in regard to the Law's purpose, constantly pointing away from the right goal to a false one, for which the Law purportedly was given. In calling for this or that to be done (e.g., You shall not steal, You shall not kill, etc.), the Law is speaking of a kind of doing that by its nature and definition proceeds from the heart and the Spirit. If now the work that is done is not of that kind, the outcome is either hypocrites (who understand the Law to mean external behavior and, if they have such behavior or work, count themselves as blameless and righteous) or people who totally despair. The Gospel, for its part, offers comfort, saying: Look, Christ is your Treasure; your Gift; your Savior, Help, and Comfort! When the heart now comes to this fork in the road between the Law and the Gospel, and sees grace here and guilt there, promise here and command there, giving here and demanding there, it refuses to go ahead; it balks. It can neither fight off the Law, nor take hold of grace. The reason is, it does not know how to divide these two words, the Law and the Gospel, from one another.

11. Where the conscience has now taken a hit, so that it well

and truly feels sin, is held fast in the grips of death, is burdened down by war, plague, poverty, disgrace, and similar disasters, and when in that case the Law announces: You belong to death; you are damned; I demand this and this from you which you have not done and cannot do; where the Law, I say, lays in with its blows and terrorizes a person with the fear of death and hell and despair, then it is high time to know how to divide the Law and the Gospel from one another, and to show each to its proper place. Here let him divide who can; this is the critical time for dividing.

12. To this moment belongs what St. Paul says: "Before faith came, we were confined under the law, kept under restraint until faith should be revealed, etc." Let a Christian know, he says, how to make a distinction between the Law and the Gospel, between works and faith, especially in regard to their goals and the messages they bear. Let him counter the Law in this way: Yes, you demand much, and you consign to damnation those who are not able to give what you require. But are you also aware how far your regime is supposed to go? Have you forgotten that its time has a set limit, as St. Paul says: When faith comes the Law should cease, make no further demands, terrorize and condemn no longer?

13. Whoever does not know this or pays no attention to it loses the Gospel, and never comes to faith. That is what the devil is doing through the "enthusiasts." He mixes together Law and Promise, faith and works; tortures poor consciences; and allows them to view neither the Law nor the Gospel with proper distinction. He drives and hunts people into the Law, and lays a net for them that bears the name: "I must do this; I must not do that." If at this point I fail to distinguish well Moses and Christ, I cannot be free, I cannot escape, I must end in despair.

14. But if I knew how to divide the Law and the Gospel rightly, there would be no need for despair. I could say: Has God given us only one kind of word, namely, the Law? Has he not also commanded the Gospel of grace and forgiveness of sins to be preached? Yes, if the conscience raises its voice where there is no faith in the

promise, the Law quickly presses its claim: You were commanded to do this and this; you have not done it; therefore you must pay the penalty. In that kind of struggle and death agony it is high and urgent time for faith to play the part of a man, to stand up without flinching, confront the Law, and address it with calm courage: My Friend Law, are you the only Word of God? Is not the Gospel, too, the Word of God? Has the Promise come to an end? Has God's mercy stopped? Or have the two—Law and Gospel, merit and grace—now been concocted into a stew and become One Thing? We will not have a God who can no longer give the Law; be assured of that. So too do we want the Law to be unmingled with the Gospel. Allow us, then, to have this distinction without let or hindrance: that you press for duty and justice, while the Gospel points us to pure grace and gift.

15. If the Law then accuses me of failing to do this or that, of being a law-breaker and a sinner in God's record book of guilt, I have to confess that it is all true. But what it says after that, "Therefore you are condemned"—that I must not concede, but resist it with firm faith and say: "According to the Law, which reckons up my guilt, I am indeed a poor, condemned sinner. But I appeal from the Law to the Gospel; because God has given another word that is higher than the Law. That word is the Gospel, which gives us, as a free gift, God's grace, the forgiveness of sins, eternal righteousness, and life. It gives you pardon and absolution from your terrors and damnation; it assures me that all guilt has been paid for by the Son of God, Jesus Christ himself. That is why it is so necessary that we know how to handle and steer both words properly, and watch carefully that they do not become mixed up with each other.

16. For God gave us these two different words, the Law and the Gospel—the one as well as the other. Each of the two bears his command. The Law is to demand perfect righteousness from everyone. The Gospel is to give the righteousness demanded by the Law to those who do not have it (i.e., to all people) by grace, as a gift. Whoever then has failed to satisfy the law and is in captivity in sin and

death, let him turn from the Law to the Gospel. Let him believe the preaching of Christ: that he is truly the Lamb of God who takes away the sin of the world; that he has reconciled his heavenly Father; that, as a totally free gift and by grace, he grants eternal righteousness, life and salvation to all who believe it. Let him hold fast to this preaching alone; let him call upon Christ, beg for grace and the forgiveness of sins, and firmly believe, for this great gift will be grasped alone by faith. Let him do that; and as he believes, so he will have.

17. This then is the correct distinction, and everything depends on getting it right. To preach about it or to divide with words is easy. But to put it to use, and into practice, is a high art, and hard to achieve. The papists and "enthusiasts" know nothing about it. I see in myself and others, who know perfectly how to talk about it, how hard this distinction is. It is a common art. Very quickly one learns to say that the Law is a different word and doctrine than the Gospel. But to distinguish in practice, to transpose the art into work, is toil and pain. St. Jerome wrote a great deal about it, but like a blind man writing about color. They define Law as having to be circumcised, to offer sacrifices, not to eat this and that, etc. From there they go on to make a new Law out of the Gospel, which purportedly teaches how a person should pray and fast, how you should become a monk or a nun, go to church, etc. They call that distinguishing. Yes; but more accurately call it throwing things together into the tub; they do not know themselves what they are washing. So listen to St. Paul, who teaches you that you have to come up higher than the question of being circumcised or not, etc. (which is all a part of being guarded and locked up under the Law). You must come to faith in Christ, through whom we become children of God and are saved forever. Otherwise stay in prison, under the wrath of God.

18. True it is that the Law or the Ten Commandments have not been annulled so that we are exempt from them and not allowed to have them. For Christ set us free from the curse, not from the obe-

dience of the Law. No, that is not what God wants. He wants us to keep the Commandments with total commitment and diligence; but not to put our trust in it when we have done so; or despair if we have not. See to it, then, that you distinguish the two words rightly, not giving more to the Law than its due, otherwise you lose the Gospel. Likewise you should not look at the Gospel or build thoughts upon it as though the Law had collapsed. Rather, let each of them remain in its own circle and sphere. Just as one must not preach that either the civil government or the pulpit should be abolished; but instead distinguish both kinds of persons and offices, and let each stick to its role and attend to it—the civil authority in accord with its territorial rights, as far as they extend; the preacher in accordance with his teaching office. I do not push myself into the mayor's office, but I keep away from it, as summer from winter. For my office is to preach, baptize, lead souls to heaven, give comfort to poor, afflicted hearts, etc. It belongs to the civil authority, on the other hand, to keep the peace, so that our young people are brought up in the fear and discipline of God. On the other hand neither the prince nor the mayor can expect to attend to the preaching, study theology, or comfort the people with God's Word.

19. So what is important is correct distinction. Not like the pope does, who is neither house dog nor hound, neither prince or bishop, yet wants to be both, and covers up his shame with both monks' and politicians' headgear. His bishops do the same thing, though they too are neither bishops nor princes. But this is what you should do: When you find yourself under attack, with the Law threatening to damn you, know that God has not given only the Law, but also a far higher Word, the blessed Gospel of Christ. If the two of them, the Law and the Gospel, now come into confrontation, and the Law finds me, a sinner, and accuses and condemns me, while the Gospel says (Matt. 9:2), "Be of good cheer, your sins are forgiven; you shall be saved": which one should I follow? Both are God's Word. St. Paul teaches you the answer: "Now that faith has come, we are no longer under a custodian." So this is where the Law stops. For

it shall and must be that the lesser word yields and gives way to the Gospel. Both are the Word of God: the Law and the Gospel. But they are not both alike. One is lower, the other higher. One is weaker, the other stronger. One is less, the other greater. If they now wrestle with one another, I follow the Gospel and say goodbye to the Law. It is better not to know the Law, than to lose the Gospel.

20. It is like what you have to do under the Law when God commands (Exodus 20:7), "You shalt not misuse my name" etc., but your prince or your parents command you to disavow God or his Gospel. God says, "Honor my name," and the Law says, "You shall love God more than your neighbor." Here I should let the lesser command (obedience to men) go by the board and keep the higher command of the First Table (which ought to be the master of all the others) and obey it alone. Far more, then, must I hold to the same principle when the Law tries to press me to desert Christ and his gift and his Gospel. In that situation I let the Law go, and I say: Dear Law, if I have failed to do your works, you do them. I am not going to allow myself to be tortured to death on your account and be taken captive and held under you, and thereby forget the Gospel. Whether I have sinned, done wrong, or not done wrong, I leave that for you, Law, to worry about. Be gone with you and leave my heart in peace; in this matter I do not know you. If you want to demand and have it that I live a godly life here on earth, I will gladly do so. But if you want to climb up and break in on me so that I lose what has been given me, then I would much rather not know you at all than lose the gift.

21. Paul is teaching us this distinction when he states that the Law performed the service of keeping us under restraint, etc. It is needed, too, to restrain and to coerce children and rude people. They need its words: You shall honor your father and your mother; you shall not commit adultery; you shall not steal or kill, etc. For the Old Adam has to be bound and held captive under the Law, which restrains us, drives us, and makes demands on us in order to keep us from a self-willed, wanton life. But that kind of compulsion

and restraint should last only until the Gospel has appeared and it is made known that we are to believe in Christ. At that point I say: On your way, Law; I am no longer willing to be held captive by you in my heart, so that I place my trust in having done this or that, or despair through not having done it. Faith is here giving me a sermon from heaven, the Gospel: that the Law no longer can or ought to torment contrite and broken hearts; it has tortured and locked up enough of them already. Therefore make room now for the Gospel, which offers and gives us God's grace and mercy.

22. That now is the picture that St. Paul sees in Christendom; and it accords well with the two words and their nature that we distinguish them and that we also soon distinguish their fruits (i.e., what each of them produces or accomplishes). Their fruits are of two kinds: taking and giving; terrifying and giving joy. The Law makes demands of us and terrifies us. The Gospel gives to us, and consoles. But then to go on from there and make use of this distinction, to put it to work when the two words, Law and Gospel, are battling head to head in your conscience; that you are then and there able to separate them rightly and to say: I am going to have these two words unmingled, with each one shown to its own place, with its own strengths: the Law for the Old Adam, the Gospel for my timid and terrified conscience (for I do not need anyone to drive me to do good works; much less can I bear the Law's accusations, being already not only harshly accused but convicted by my own conscience; rather I need comfort and help from the Gospel of Jesus Christ)—to do this now is very hard, especially with the Law wanting to get my conscience into its shackles. See to it, then, that you take hold of the Promise, and do not let the Law get the upper hand or rule in your conscience and so bring you into judgment, for that would be a denial of the Gospel. Instead you must swing yourself right around and take hold of the grace word, the Gospel of the forgiveness of sins: that God has also commanded the Gospel to be preached to the poor, in which his will is not to play a game with you on the grounds of justice, but to deal with you by his grace as a

kindly father does toward his children when they are in need: that he wills to forgive you by grace for everything that you have failed to do, and to give you as a gift what you are unable to do.

23. Thus the Law should apply its strength toward external discipline alone, and leave undisturbed the little room where the Gospel wills to dwell, as St. Paul says, "Before faith came, we were confined under the Law." Therefore another word must come, in addition to the Law and over it, namely, the Gospel, which sets us into a godliness not our own, one that is outside of us, in Christ alone. For it is impossible for us to become righteous through the Law, because even in the past the Law attempted far more than it accomplished. Hence it is also undeniable that no human being can become godly and righteous through the work of the Law. For if that were possible, it would long since have happened. Therefore another, higher Word belongs here, which is the Gospel and faith in Christ, as is heard. God give us grace and strengthen our faith. Amen!

NOTES

1. Martin Luther, "The Distinction between Law and Gospel: A Sermon by Martin Luther," trans. Willard L. Burce, *Concordia Journal* 18 (April 1992): 153–63. For the German original of this sermon, see either the Weimar Edition (36:8–42) or the St. Louis Edition (9:799–811) of *Luther's Works*.